# MYSTERIES
# OF THE VENUS
# PENTAGRAM

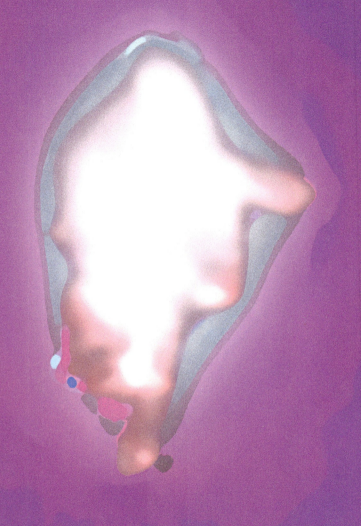

Photograph by Tashi Powers
www.enlighteningtimes.com

Photo editing by Darius Gottlieb
CelloHeart@gmail.com

# MYSTERIES
# OF THE VENUS
# PENTAGRAM

Written by Tashi Powers
Evolutionary Astrologer

Designed by George Ozuna

Independently Published 2018

© Tashi Grady Powers 2018
FIRST EDITION

Independently Published
California, United States of America

For information on this and other works visit
www.enlighteningtimes.com

*This book is dedicated to:* Nicolaus Copernicus,
Giordano Bruno,
Galileo Galilei,
Johannes Kepler,
Dane Rudhyar,
Jeffrey Wolf Green

# TABLE OF CONTENTS

Photograph by Tashi Powers
www.enlighteningtimes.com

Photo editing by Darius Gottlieb
CelloHeart@gmail.com

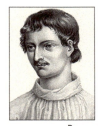

| Copernicus | Bruno | Galileo |
|:---:|:---:|:---:|
| 1473-1543 | 1548-1600 | 1564-1642 |

## DEDICATION

With the development of the telescope in the 1600s our astronomers began to study the planet Venus more closely. And yet, were we to give credit where credit is due, we should pay homage to the ancient Babylonian astrologers who had already made a study of Venus's rise and set, as evidenced on the *Venus Tablet* of *Ammisaduqa*, dated back to 700 BC.

First let us acknowledge Johannes Kepler who became the first person to predict a *Transit of Venus* in 1627. He forecast the *Transit of Venus* 1631 event. Kepler died in 1630 without realizing the event was not visible in Europe.

In progressive England, the first recorded modern observation of a *Transit of Venus* was made by Jeremiah Horrocks on the 24 November 1639. And intriguing to note that both Queen Elizabeth I (7 Sep 1533–24 Mar 1603) and King James I (19 Jun 1566–27 Mar 1625) were Rosicrucian mystics. Each monarch also consulted astrologers, Jon Dee and Tycho Brahee and others, who had the favor of the Royal Court!

Kepler
1571-1630

Dane Rudhyar
1895-1985

Jeffrey Wolf Green
12/02/46-Present

Galileo furthered his theories of Heliocentrism during the *Transit of Venus*—1631-1639. So, we are all beholden to these men on whose shoulders we stand as we continue to discover the truth about the mysterious pentagrams of Venus.

Galileo died under house arrest in 1642 because he would not recant his theories of Heliocentrism. He had discovered what Copernicus and Kepler knew, that the Earth and the planets revolve around the Sun at the center of the Solar System, through the observation of the cycles of Venus.

On February 17, 1600, Giordano Bruno was burned at the stake, as he defied the church's censorship. Bruno, Galileo and Copernicus were all persecuted for discovering Natural Law.

The last *Transits of Venus* in 2004 and 2012, both of which were visible, connect us all back to these justly-famous Astrologers.

And our current *Transit of Venus* has ignited a great interest in Her Natural Laws, but thankfully we are not

Venus Tablet of Ammisaduqa 720-740 BC Stone

being burned at the stake for the enormous reforms we are undergoing. Instead, we're exceedingly fortunate to study the work of contemporary astrological visionary, Jeffrey Wolf Green.

I dedicate this book to this modern-day reformer JWG and the work he has done to revolutionize astrology, just like Galileo, Kepler and Copernicus. His work is bold and deep and profound. All of us now have the ability to benefit from Jeffrey's EA Paradigm, and in so doing we are able to learn Natural Law. As we realize self-empowerment we are able to now share that gift with others—as we move from lack to satisfaction. We can now apply the EA principles of sharing, caring and inclusion using astrological timing to evolve in alignment with Natural Law.

This book is a study of the Natural Laws of the Planet Venus, as we begin to look deeper into her cycles—using modern technology. I am dedicated to a rebirth of God/dess energy, on so many fronts.

March 19, 2018—Published after a New Capricorn VPP formed on my Descendant, and after the Total Full Moon Leo—Aquarius Eclipse. And, of course on the New Venus-Moon, First Gate of the Evening Star. ☯

## INTRODUCTION
by Linda Jonson, Evolutionary Astrologer

Have you heard of the Venus Star and wondered how you would go about incorporating the deeper meaning of its symbolism into the personal relationships in your life?

With interpretations and analysis distilled from the collective wisdom of our great Evolutionary Astrologers —Jeffrey Wolf Green, Deva Green, Dane Rudhyar—as well as Melanie Reinhardt, Tashi Powers presents a comprehensive key to unravelling the meanings of the Venus Pentagram Mandala in this thought-provoking and illuminating guide to the expanse of the heart.

Tashi Powers wrote this book because of her great love for astrology. She is dedicating this book to her beloved teacher, the founder of Evolutionary Astrology, Jeffrey Wolf Green.

You can now discover new ways to bring illumination to the whole area of love (both inner and outer sides of Venus) and relationships. You will learn how to integrate the deeper cycles of Venus, and master the essential techniques of the Venus Pentagram Mandala.

Inside each chapter you will find all the tools you need:

Venus cycles, Pentagram points, Star Dates, Venus Retrograde and Direct, Morning Star and Evening Star, Heroes journeys, transit information, example charts, correlations to world events, diagrams, tables, keywords, and symbology.

Provided at the end is a special section—The Venus Through The Signs Workbook—to help you observe, correlate, and journal your experiences of the phases and movements of the Venus Star in your life, and in the lives of your friends and lovers.

Tashi Powers, with passion, attention, and patience, has provided for the first time, rich meanings of all Venus Pentagram points in conjunction with her strong foundation in Evolutionary Astrology principles. Here are the essential tools that will open up new ground to understanding the life-enriching messages of the benefic Venus Star in your life.

So turn the page and begin now! ☯

Photograph by Tashi Powers
www.enlighteningtimes.com

Photo editing by Darius Gottlieb
CelloHeart@gmail.com

## Acknowledgments

I wouldn't have been able to write this, my first book, without my gifted and talented Graphics Designer George Ozuna. George has one of his Venus Pentagram Mandala Points on his natal Venus. I think his beautiful artwork speaks to the Aries Kumari Kiss that his Venus received and he nourished, and now flourishes in his work as an artist.

My outstanding line editor, Darius Gottlieb, a poet in his own right, also gave me amazing images and an overview of the work for which I am deeply grateful.

John Nelson edited the book and faithfully advised & cheered me onto completion. The painstaking work it takes to edit a book is Herculean and the old saying, all good writing is re-writing could not have been truer. I am deeply grateful.

My daughter Madison has been a source of enormous strength and love these past few years as Pluto opposed my Gemini stellium and headed for my Capricorn stellium. This combination released all that I was outgrowing, pulling one carpet after another out from under me, until I found my way to my resolution node—Uranus conjunct the South Node—and began writing books on evolutionary astrology. I could not have accomplished this feat without her enduring love and support.

My Nine Treasures Yoga community in Los Angeles and my friends and students, with whom I meditate, pray, and do yoga, are a constant joy and encourage me to teach and help humanity.

My Kundalini Yoga teacher Tej Kaur Khalsa inspires me to meditate daily, to keep up, go high and wide, work on myself and help others.

I am grateful for my Malibu community at Olandar, where I teach regularly with artist Leigh McCloskey whose artwork appears in this book. We are all enlightened by his generous sharing of the tarot drawings. Carla and Leigh have always been my true-blue friends and support my EA classes.

I am deeply grateful to Linda Jonson and the EA Zoom meetings that are also a source of great joy and fellowship.

And to my students and clients whose puzzles we solve; I cherish your depth of trust and faith in my ability to help.

I work to compliment the universe, humbled by the perfection of even its most challenging aspects.

And then there is this birthright, these angels, who have been my guardian-angels since birth. I have given them nicknames: Florinda and Gregory.

There are pictures of them I was able to take with my i-Phone sprinkled throughout the book. I am not sure why I am able to show them to you, as Angels prefer to be invisible, but I captured them as they flew in a few times.

They love me unconditionally, help me tirelessly, and guide me unsparingly. Their guidance is like a crystal fire, a lightning of light that showers down from an etheric plane.

Their touch is blinding, comforting, electrifying and sometimes bewildering, but I wouldn't have come here without their support. Their love feels like the Kumari Kiss, and this book would not be happening without their presence.

Finally I want to thank my 9th house Part of Fortune, that I trust granted these teachers: Jeffrey Wolf Green, Dane Rudhyar and Joseph Campbell who all shared the spark of inspiration they each received, with me. ☯

Photograph by Tashi Powers
www.enlighteningtimes.com

Photo editing by Darius Gottlieb
CelloHeart@gmail.com

## PART ONE
## HOW TO USE THE BOOK

Get an overview of the Venus Pentagram Mandala by reading the first part of the book.

We have provided a workbook page section at the back of the book to work with your Venus Pentagram Points.

Add all your natal chart positions to the workbook.

You will find the Seven Gates of the Venus Ascent & Descent that you can journal in the workbook.

This book contains the modernization of the myths about the Descent of Venus, and many ways to interact with the movement of the Sun, Moon & Venus. ☯

Earth Venus 8 Orbits

# THE FIERY PENTAGRAMS

The stylized diagram of the 5 sequential Venus cycles shown here form a pentagram made by the 5 points of its Sun-Venus conjunctions. This is a symbol found in ancient Vedic mythology and all mystical traditions.

In the Vedic Astrological lore, the Holy Kumaris are considered Promethean beings—who were thought to have used these Sun-Venus conjunctions to give infant humanity the spark of intelligence and the seed of individuality—for better and for worse.

In Natural Law, the Venus Pentagram Points (VPP) are empowering points of intelligence in your chart. These Venus-Sun conjunctions in your personal horoscope highlight the place where you nurture the Kumari seeds, which are regularly bestowed via transits into your chart.

This Link has a beautiful rendition of the pattern—that Venus and the Earth make moving around the Sun— forming the Venus Pentagram Mandala. 🌀

*https://astrobutterfly.com/2017/03/22/venus-conjunct-sun-a-new-venus-cycle-a-rebirth-of-the-hearth/*

# Venus & The Holy Kumari

"The Fiery Pentagrams" signify the empowering rays of higher love—to be used for evolution—are now easy to plot. Using modern technology, we can isolate the five points on a pentagram that form a unique mandala for you.

The five signs of your Mandala correspond to eight-year periods in which these same five signs are repeated. There are also years when the signs change, and these are break-out changing years in society and human life.

The Gnostics represented this pentagram as the fiery body of the Holy Spirit. So, whatever you want to call it in Natural Law, it is an empowering point of intelligence. It is a part of Mother Nature's Cosmic clock. Venus—in to relationship with the Sun and Earth—makes these pentagrams. I see them as points in your chart that are regularly infused with Venusian fire.

These are in your natal horoscope and are a part of your own personal mandala of being. They are also a part of the mandala of humanity; the Venus Pentagram Points show the path of evolution.

Use your own Venus Pentagram Star to discover where you are in this unfolding spiral that is a "process of being." 🌀

### Plot your VPP using these links:

https://sophiavenus.com/pdf/FindYourVenusStarPoint.pdf
https://eclipse.gsfc.nasa.gov/transit/catalog/VenusCatalog.html

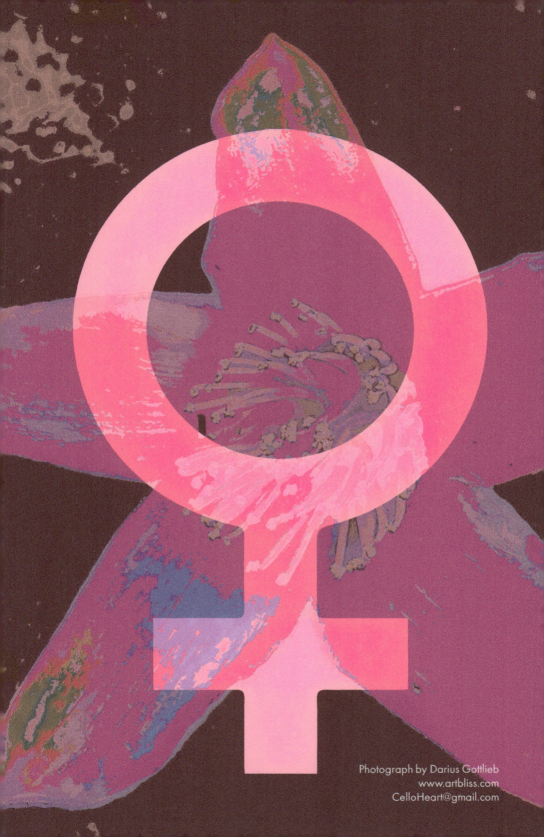

Photograph by Darius Gottlieb
www.artbliss.com
CelloHeart@gmail.com

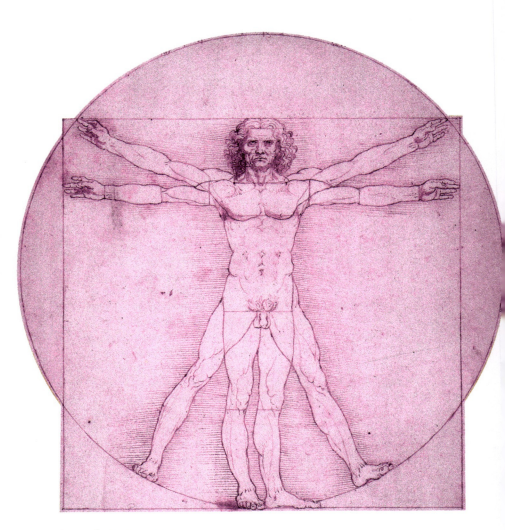

Leonardo Da Vinci 1490
Drawing

# THE VITRUVIAN MAN

The Venus 5 Pentagram Points have been connected to the Vitruvian Man.

See how the drawing, by philosopher and artist Leonardo Da Vinci, seems to portray the Five-Pointed Star.

Perhaps Leonardo Da Vinci, a Rosicrucian, was portraying a heliocentric-based universe when he created L'Uomo Vitruviano around 1490 during the Italian Renaissance.

The drawing, which is in pen and ink on paper, depicts a man in two superimposed positions with his arms and legs apart and inscribed in a circle and square. ☯

Source: Wikipedia

Datura Flower by Darius Gottlieb
www.artbliss.com

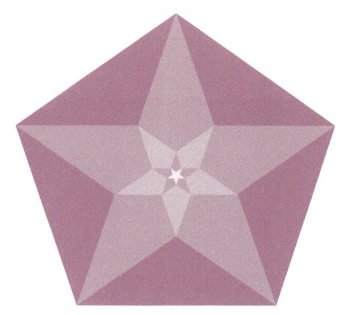

Illustration by George Ozuna

# GEOMETRIC PENTAGRAMS
## FOUND IN NATURE

It regenerates itself, creating one pentagram after another inside itself. By joining all five points of the pentagram, a new pentagram forms in the middle, and this goes on forever—forming the Venus Pentagram Mandala.

How eternal and regenerative is our love force?
The more love we give, the more we receive.

Each Sun-Venus Pentagram Point (VPP) affords another chance to generate and regenerate the following Venusian principles:

Love, Self-Worth, Relating, Financial Well Being, Economic Reform, Societal Mores, New Influences In Our World, New Values That Move Humanity Forward...

Venus in the sky at Night

# Natural Laws of the Venus Cycles

## SUPERIOR CONJUNCTION
The Venus-Sun Superior Conjunction occurs when Venus is behind the Sun. Venus is moving in Direct motion.

## INFERIOR CONJUNCTION
The Venus-Sun Inferior Conjunction occurs when Venus is between the Earth and the Sun. Venus is moving in Retrograde motion. In both cases Venus is not visible.

## MAXIMUM ELONGATION
Occurs 216 days after the Superior Conjunction

## MAXIMUM BRIGHTNESS
Occurs 36 days following maximum elongation

The Venus Pentagram Points form a Pentagram Star that revolves within an oval in a clockwise direction. The pentagram is formed after 5 cycles of Venus-Sun conjunctions in approximately 8 year cycles.

Venus-Sun Conjunctions repeat in five-cycle sets completing an entire round once every 1,215 years.
These long cycles are called The *Transit of Venus*, and show major historic changes as our tools and values both evolve during the *Transit of Venus* over the Sun.

## Examples of the last Transit of Venus:
English Renaissance 1630s
Industrial Revolution/America 1760s
Telephone Invented 1880
Internet goes global 2004-2012
The next *Transit of Venus* occurs in 2117.

Venus Pentagram Trajectory
Illustration by George Ozuna

# Venus Synodic Cycles

Venus phenomenon occurs in multiples of 36 days

1. **INFERIOR CONJUNCTION—RX—MORNING STAR**

2. **GREATEST BRIGHTNESS**—occurs 36 days later

3. **GREATEST ELONGATION**—occurs 36 days later

4. **SUPERIOR CONJUNCTION—DIRECT—EVENING STAR** occurs 6 x 36 (216) days after Greatest Elongation

5. **GREATEST ELONGATION**—occurs 6 x 36 (216) days after the Superior Conjunction

6. **GREATEST BRIGHTNESS**—occurs 36 days later

7. **INFERIOR CONJUNCTION**—happens 36 days later

8. **SOLAR GLARE**—At the Inferior Conjunction, Venus is lost in the Solar Glare. When Venus reaches Superior Conjunction, she is behind the Sun and once again Venus is lost in the Solar Glare. Occasionally however Venus will move widely north of the sun. The tilt of Venus will cause her to appear as both evening star and morning star and the Solar Glare is of a shorter period.

## PART TWO
## VENUS PENTAGRAM POINTS

Using modern technology, the Venus Pentagram Points can now be easily plotted, so that we can study historic events.

The five current VPPs are discussed in this chapter, and we have given you some historic charts that are connected to the VPP. We can now see that Martin Luther King's enduring speech was given on the same day a new VPP formed. What a Kumari Kiss that has been!

Keep an eye on the changing VPP every 9 months, and see how it brings people and new values into our world.

The VPP also changes the social climate around us, and these big changes are part of at least an eight-year cycle. We can also get an overview of how the changes in our world unfold slowly as the VPP Mandala receives its many Sun-fired Kumari Kisses over the longer cycles of the Venus Transit. ☯

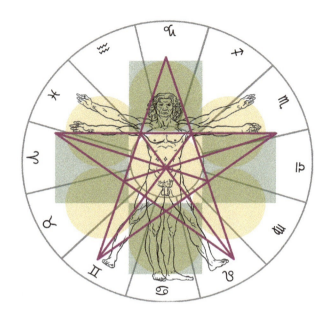

JAN 09 2018 **SUPERIOR CONJUNCTION** 18° Cap 57'

OCT 26 2018 **INFERIOR CONJUNCTION** 3° Sc 06'

AUG 14 2019 **SUPERIOR CONJUNCTION** 21° Leo 11'

JUL 03 2020 **INFERIOR CONJUNCTION** 13° Gem 36'

MAR 26 2021 **SUPERIOR CONJUNCTION** 5° Ar 50'

# CURRENT
## VENUS PENTAGRAM POINT DATES

We share so many of the VPPs in common that I am not sure they solely define us personally. The Kumari Kiss of the VPP complexity describes a larger unfolding.

Modern use of technology and the computer allow us to observe and mathematically track the enduring mysteries of Venus's magnetic spirals and patterns. Please take a look at your leisure at the tables enclosed of currently notated astronomical phenomenon of the *Transit of Venus*.

Use the transiting VPP to watch unfolding events, and to see how the VPP connects to changing values and morality. It may also foreshadow individuals who will show up in your life. The natal VPP will be activated by the transiting Venus Fiery Pentagram.

The current VPP at 18 Capricorn formed on Jan 09 2018 and it was conjunct the North Node of Pluto. Certainly, the events connected to this event will be easier to understand as time passes.

Jeffrey Wolf Green spoke at length in various videos which can be found on YouTube, about the tumultuous period of Pluto's transit through Capricorn. Pluto is also transiting its own North Node during 2018-2019, and it is likely the Kumari Kiss will cause a huge reform.

The Capricorn VPP could also point to political reform. The following VPP is in Scorpio in October of 2018. This Scorpio VPP is ending on Oct 23 2026, at 00°Scorpio 45' Rx. The next VPP BEGINS IN 2022 at 29 Libra. This happens before the Scorpio one fades out, so expect some intensity as the power struggles fade to co-operation in all levels of life.

| | | | | | | | | | | | |
|---|---|---|---|---|---|---|---|---|---|---|---|
| 8 YEAR TRANSIT OF VENUS | | | | 8 YEAR TRANSIT OF VENUS | | | | 8 YEAR TRANSIT OF VENUS | | | |
| DEC 07, 1631 | DEC 04, 1639 | JUN 06, 1761 | JUN 03, 1769 | DEC 09, 1874 | DEC 06, 1882 | JUN 08, 2004 | JUN 06, 2012 | DEC 11, 2117 | DEC 06, 2125 | JUN 06, 2247 | JUN 06, 2255 |
| | | 8 YEAR TRANSIT OF VENUS | | | | 8 YEAR TRANSIT OF VENUS | | | | 8 YEAR TRANSIT OF VENUS | |
| | | | 243 YEARS | | | | | | | | |
| | | | | | 243 YEARS | | | | | | |
| | 243 YEARS | | | | | | 243 YEARS | | | | |

The rare 243-year Venus Transit cycles have two occurrences of the major alignment of Venus with her Nodes. The Sun Venus Transits are shown below. The last Venus Transit pair occurred in 1874 and 1882. We are living in historic times, as we have experienced the current Venus Transit from 2004-2012.

The Transit occurs again in 2117 and 2125. ☯

Pallas Athena Rose by Darius Gottlieb
www.artbliss.com

# TRANSITIONAL
## PENTAGRAM STAR DATES

**2018-2022**—will be transitional times as the Scorpio Pentagram Prevailing Star point shifts to a Libra Pentagram Head Star.

**Jun 22 1960**—the last Cancer star at 01°Cancer 13'D

**Jun 19 1964**—the new star began at 28°Gemini 38'RX MS

**Jan 21 1982**—the last Aquarius star began at 01°Aquarius 52'D on Feb 18, 1890 ES

**Jan 19 1986**—the new Capricorn star began at 29°Capricorn 17'D ES

**Aug 24 1983**—the last Virgo star at 01°Virgo 25'R began Sep 23, 1875 as an Evening Star

**Aug 23 1987**—the new Leo star began at 29°Leo 36'D

**Oct 26 2018**—the fading Scorpio Star at 03°Scorpio 06'R began Nov 21, 1926 as an Evening Star

**Oct 22 2022**—the new Libra Star at 29°Libra 26'D Evening Star

**Oct 23 2026**—the last Scorpio Star at 00°Scorpio 45'R ☯

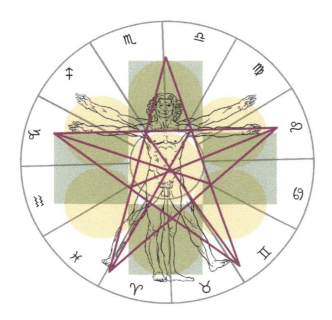

# TRANSITIONAL PENTAGRAM POINTS

On Oct 22, 2022 a New Venus Pentagram Point (VPP) will be at 29°Libra 26' as an Evening Star. Scorpio doesn't quite fade yet, as the last Scorpio VPP occurs on Oct 23, 2026, at 00°Scorpio 45' Rx. The next Libra VPP is on Oct 20, 2030 and is also a Superior Conjunction. The first Rx, Inferior Conjunction of Venus and the Sun in Libra does not occur until Oct 21, 2034 at 28 Libra 22 Rx.

It is my prayer that as the Scorpio VPP fades we will have learned lessons of sharing power and that the EA keywords of sharing, caring and inclusion will be the directive of the day. If, as Yogi Bhajan, a mystic from India, stated: "The Age of Aquarius begins in 2035," then this new VPP in Libra in 2034 is another indicator to explore.

In Libra we learn balance. Over any given lifetime we are presented with various sensate experiences, the litmus tests for all sorts of relationships and confrontations with others. Through contrast and comparisons, we eventually do learn to see the reflections of the One.

# BIRTH OF THE INTERNET
Nov 21 1969

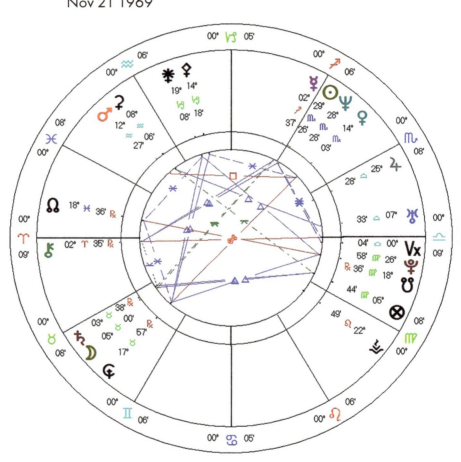

Arpnet—Nov 21, 1969 Aries wheel.

# CHANGING OF THE GUARD
## 1960s PLUTO WORLD ORDER SHIFTING

There is a changing of the guard indicated as the new Gemini Pentagram Point at 28°Gemini is retrograde and is a Morning Star that began on Jun 19, 1964 at 28°Gemini.

Historians might look at the Gemini-Venus Pentagram Point forming at the time when the people found their voice.

The Internet began in the sixties, called Arpanet during its initial development. It was invented by the Advanced Research Projects Agency (DARPA) at the U.S. Department of Defense, and then later called the Internet.

Over many decades as this gift of the Venus-Sun Gemini conjunctions unfolded, the way human beings communicate has radically evolved.

Arpnet—Nov 21, 1969 Aries wheel.
Sun-Neptune in Scorpio certainly describes the sneaky side of Arpnet and the empowering transfor-mational side of the Internet that replaced it. Venus also describes the wealth involved with the Neptune-Sun Scorpio conjunction. Pluto and the South Node indicate a collective shift.

The Venus Pentagram Point at 29°Gemini in 1969, on the galactic center indicates to me that Arpnet is the NEW KUMARI kiss for humanity. The Internet went viral on the *Transit of Venus* 2004-2012 with two VPPs in Gemini. ☯

# 1963 CIVIL RIGHTS MARCH

**Civil Rights March on Washington DC**
Aug 28, 1963—250,000 People Protested

The VPP that began in 1964 was in Gemini. Our current rare *Transit of Venus* is a part of the unfolding of the larger Gemini Venus Pentagram Points. From 2004-2012 two VPPs formed in Gemini, as Venus transited the Sun. This is part of the overall 1,215 year cycle of the Venus Transit.

# CHANGING OF THE GUARD
## 1960s PLUTO WORLD ORDER SHIFTING

The Civil Rights March on Washington, D.C. for Jobs and Freedom culminated with Dr. Martin Luther King's famous "I Have a Dream" speech from the steps of the Lincoln Memorial. Over 250,000 people participated in this march for equal rights.

"I Have a Dream" remains to this day a wake up call for an end to racism in the United States. MLK heightened national awareness for civil and economic rights, with this historical speech—a pivotal call to action for the civil rights movement.

Yet it was only a 16-minute speech, beginning at 3:00 PM and ending at 3:16!

The radical 60s correlated to the changing of the guard as the new Gemini VPP began as a Morning Star on the axis of the Galactic Center.

John F. Kennedy and Martin Luther King were both slain in the fight for equality that the Uranus-Pluto conjunction also reveals. The wounded healer, asteroid Chiron opposes the Uranus-Pluto Conjunction showing the losses. ☯

### For more information:

en.wikipedia.org/wiki/I_Have_a_Dream
*history.com/topics/black-history/march-on-washington

# 1963 "I HAVE A DREAM"

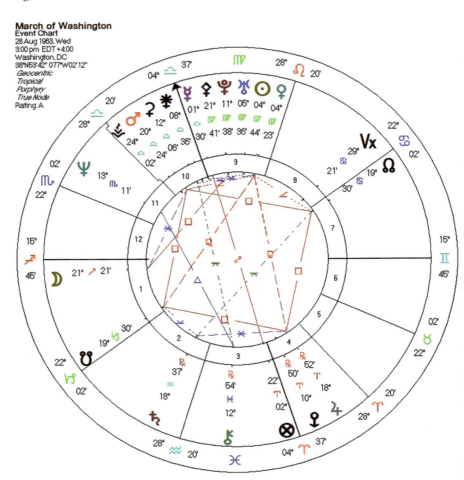

**March of Washington**
Event Chart
28 Aug 1963, Wed
3:00 pm EDT +4:00
Washington, DC
38°N53'42" 077°W02'12"
*Geocentric*
*Tropical*
*Porphyry*
*True Node*
Rating: A

## Civil Rights March on Washington DC

Aug 28 1963 3:00pm EDT

Observe that the Sun & Venus are already in the same degree at 4 Virgo. The new VPP is hours away at 05 Virgo 58 D

# CHANGING OF THE GUARD
## 1960s PLUTO URANUS PARADIGM SHIFT

In this chart, Mercury in Libra is moving toward Mars in Libra, indicative of the ability to fight and express the meaning behind the oppression of Black Americans.

Venus & Sun in Virgo conjunct Uranus & Pluto in Virgo = Revolution/Evolution.

There was a long way to go—as this chart portrays through the journey of the balsamic line up. The new Virgo VPP balsamic to Pluto shows the seeds being sowed for a new tomorrow. The protest typifies the EA keywords for the balsamic phase: "Absolute; Infinite; Timeless."

Here we see Venus Sun, Uranus, and Pluto lined up on the Virgo Pentagram Star. A New Venus Pentagram point forms a few hours later, coinciding with this event. This is a Kumari Kiss that we are still struggling to embrace. ☯

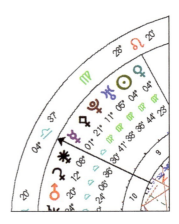

# 1989 WORLD ORDER SHIFT

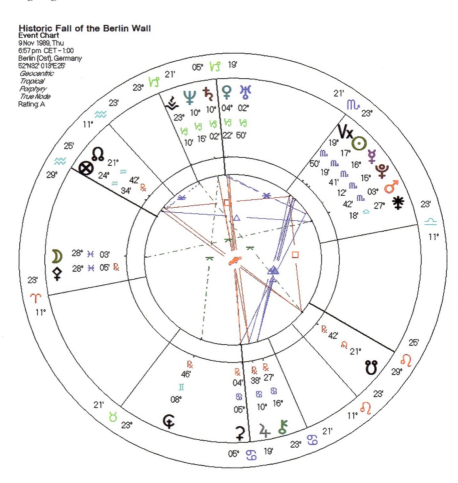

**Historic Fall of the Berlin Wall**
Event Chart
9 Nov 1989, Thu
6:57 pm CET –1:00
Berlin (Ost), Germany
52°N32' 013°E25'
*Geocentric*
*Tropical*
*Porphyry*
*True Node*
Rating: A

On Nov 09 1989, thousands of East Germans flocked to border crossings in East Berlin and for the first time they were able to cross into West Berlin.

# CHANGING OF THE GUARD
## 1980s CAPRICORN PARADIGM SHIFT

The Berlin Wall which divided the nation for almost three decades, fell as the East and West Berliners removed the barrier together.

Naturally, Pluto is involved in such a big-world-changing event. Mars is in balsamic conjunction to Pluto, while Mercury and Sun are in a new phase conjunction. Venus in a stellium with Uranus, Saturn and Neptune; all are now resonant with the new VPP in Capricorn.

Saturn conjunct Neptune is an "architecture archetype." Neptune can also dissolve a structure. Uranus is famous for freedom from the known.

**Jan 21 1982**—Last Aquarius Star D, began Feb 18 1890 ES

**Aug 24 1983**—Last Virgo Star Rx, began Sep 23 1875 ES

**Jan 19 1986**—New Capricorn star 29°Cap 17'D ES

**Aug 23 1987**—New Leo star at 29°LEO 36'D ES

**1987**—End of the Cold War

**1989**—Fall of Berlin Wall = 29°Capricorn VPP

**1991**—Dissolution of The Soviet Union

**1993**—Birth of International Islamic Terrorism ☯

## PART THREE:
### ARCHETYPES & THE VPP

In Part Three the intent is to empower you, the reader, with aspects of ancient archetypal wisdom.

Myth and Tarot have informed Astrology for aeons of thousands of years, and may indeed be the Mother of Astrology.

These images are offered here, along with EA quotes from The School of Evolutionary Astrology's Glossary, to help deepen our grasp of the Natural Law that is at the heart of everything. ☯

# Empress Rules Venus

*Excerpt from Leigh McCloskey*

The Empress is the 3rd key in the Tarot Arcana and is represented astrologically by the planet Venus. The Empress symbolizes mother nature, the fullness of fertility, growth, prosperity, peace and beauty. She is creative inspiration and the guardian of true magic.

To her belong love, beauty, art, imagination, intuition, sensuality, and desire. She symbolizes love as the formative energy of the universe. She is the sustaining and nurturing mother of all creation. Luminous intelligence is the mode of consciousness attributed to the Empress. She is known as the mother of light, the mother of ideas, described as pure emotion having no subject or object, being filled with and emanating light. She is the passageway between luminous light and the unknowable, supreme darkness. ☯

TAROT-EMPRESS—Sophia / The Great Mother—Key #3
One of 22 original pen and ink drawings by Leigh J McCloskey from his masterwork of original art & writing, "Tarot ReVisioned," (Olandar Press 2003)

# HIGH PRIESTESS RULES MOON
*Excerpt from Leigh McCloskey*

The High Priestess is the 2nd Key in the Tarot Arcana. Her path is associated astrologically with the Moon. She represents the waters of pure consciousness. Her dominion is absolute depth. ☯

**Nota Bene: The Moon and Venus conjoin over seven months.**

**Pay attention to the lessons. EA teaches that it is through the Moon that we experience the depth of emotional experiences that help us evolve. Whether it is facing repression, or celebrating self-sufficiency, we must embrace all of our emotions.**

**Ultimately the Moon's Archetype corresponds to happiness and joy. Perhaps Venus in sunlight is a reflection of this joy.**

TAROT—HIGH PRIESTESS—Key #2
One of 22 original pen and ink drawings by Leigh J McCloskey from his masterwork of original art & writing, "Tarot ReVisioned,"
(Olandar Press 2003)

# The World Rules Capricorn
*Excerpt from Leigh McCloskey*

The World is the 21st Key in the Tarot Arcana and is represented astrologically by the planet Saturn.

Saturn is associated with time, maturity, structure, gravitation, boundaries, the truth about the truth, and beauty through perfection.

The mode of consciousness attributed to the World archetype is administrative intelligence, suggesting that it guides and directs the energies of manifestation, formalizing patterns that govern life and order creation.

**Nota Bene: Capricorn is one the five current VPPs. We are therefore involved in extracting ourselves from the domination/submission paradigms in both our personal and collective world.**

**PLUTO IN CAPRICORN 2008-2022.** ☯

TAROT—THE WORLD—Key #21
One of 22 original pen and ink drawings by Leigh J McCloskey from his masterwork of original art & writing, "Tarot ReVisioned,"
(Olandar Press 2003)

Find the Pentagram Point closest to your birth year, month and day. Place the current VPP into your natal chart. The house in which it is located will show you how the Venus-Sun-Earth Inferior or Superior Conjunction is working in your life. All five of the Pentagram points are attractors, and they will line up with important events and in the charts of those individuals with whom you share the journey of life. Venus's Pentagram Star Point in Capricorn correlates to your intention to be responsible. Its position can indicate the arena where you must take a leadership role.

# THE CAPRICORN
## PENTAGRAM STAR DATES

| | |
|---|---|
| Jan 19 1986 | 29°Cp17' D ES |
| Jan 18 1990 | 28°Cp35' R |
| Jan 16 1994 | 26°Cp43' D |
| Jan 16 1998 | 26°Cp07' R |
| Jan 14 2002 | 24°Cp07' D |
| Jan 13 2006 | 23°Cp40' R |
| Jan 11 2010 | 21°Cp32' D |
| Jan 11 2014 | 21°Cp11' R |
| Jan 09 2018 | 18°Cp57' D |
| Jan 08 2022 | 18°Cp43' R |
| Jan 06 2026 | 16°Cp22' D |
| Jan 06 2030 | 16°Cp15' R |
| Jan 03 2034 | 13°Cp46' D |
| Jan 03 2038 | 13°Cp46' R |

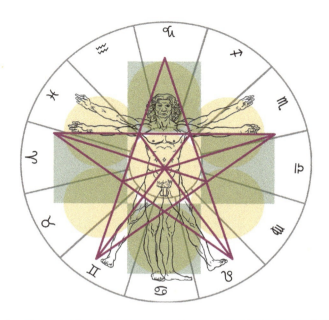

# THE CAPRICORN PENTAGRAM STAR

*Capricorn is one half of the Cancer/Capricorn polarity. Capricorn is the objective side. The Venus Pentagram point will show us by house placement where we need to mature and what kind of work we need to do.*

*We might also study it to see which arena we would be valued in positions of leadership.*

*Capricorn is the sign that relates to both inner and outer authority. Once we establish our inner knowing of right work we develop our mastery, and often others will give us acceptance and authority. Saturn and Capricorn represent time. Your connections to this VPP might bring opportunity to help you accomplish the tasks your soul wishes you to complete.*

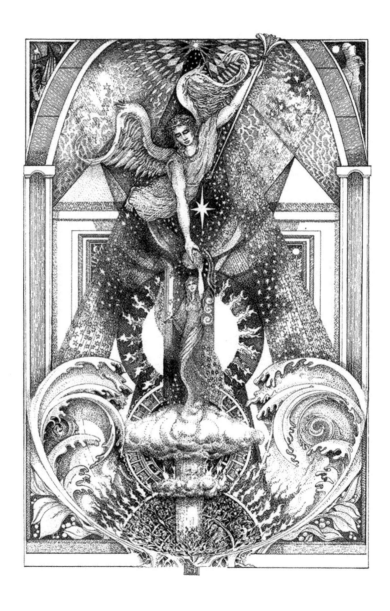

# JUDGEMENT RULES SCORPIO-PLUTO
*Excerpt from Leigh McCloskey*

Judgement is the 20th key in the Tarot Arcana and is represented astrologically by the planet Pluto. Pluto is associated with transformation, the unknowable depths of the unconscious, and mass events.

The Hebrew letter Shin, is the archetype attributed to Judgement, whose symbol is a tooth, or fang. It functions as incisiveness, having the power to penetrate the illusion of separateness and the limitations of form. Tradition suggests that the letter Shin is life-breath of the divine ones or holy spirit, therefore it is considered the holy letter.

The mode of consciousness attributed to Judgement is perpetual intelligence, which elucidates the fact that the intelligent guiding principle behind manifestation is constant. External forms emerge, develop, and decay, a cycle affecting not simply individual existence, but also the life and death of civilizations.

**Nota Bene: Pluto is at the core of the EA paradigm. Please read the EA glossary to associate Pluto with the VPP study. Refer to JWG's EA Glossary to help you understand the depth of Pluto as it may relate to the VPP.** ☯

TAROT—JUDGEMENT—Key #20
One of 22 original pen and ink drawings by Leigh J McCloskey from his masterwork of original art & writing, "Tarot ReVisioned,"
(Olandar Press 2003)

Find the Pentagram Point closest to your birth year, month and day. Place the current VPP into your natal chart. The house in which it is located will show you how the Venus-Sun-Earth Inferior or Superior Conjunction is working in your life. All five of the Pentagram points are attractors, and they will line up with important events and in the charts of those individuals with whom you share the journey of life. Venus's Pentagram Point in Aries correlates to your fierce desire to express yourself and where you will need to find healthy ways to value your need to do your own thing.

# THE SCORPIO
## PENTAGRAM STAR DATES

| | |
|---|---|
| Nov 21 1926 | 28°Sc26' D ES |
| Nov 22 1930 | 29°Sc44' R |
| Nov 18 1934 | 25°Sc59' D |
| Nov 20 1938 | 27°Sc16' R |
| Nov 16 1942 | 23°Sc30' D |
| Nov 17 1946 | 24°Sc50' R |
| Nov 13 1950 | 21°Sc02' D |
| Nov 15 1954 | 22°Sc23' R |
| Nov 11 1958 | 18°Sc36' D |
| Nov 12 1962 | 19°Sc57' R |
| Nov 08 1966 | 16°Sc09' D |
| Nov 10 1970 | 17°Sc32' R |
| Nov 06 1974 | 13°Sc44' D |
| Nov 07 1978 | 15°Sc07' R |
| Nov 03 1982 | 11°Sc19' D |
| Nov 05 1986 | 12°Sc42' R |
| Nov 01 1990 | 08°Sc56' D |
| Nov 02 1994 | 10°Sc18' R |
| Oct 29 1998 | 06°Sc32' D |
| Oct 31 2002 | 07°Sc53' R |
| Oct 27 2006 | 04°Sc10' D |
| Oct 28 2010 | 05°Sc30' R |
| Oct 25 2014 | 01°Sc48' D |
| Oct 26 2018 | 03°Sc06' R |
| | |
| Oct 22 2022 | 29°Li26' D ES |

# THE SCORPIO PENTAGRAM STAR

*Scorpio is one half of the Taurus/Scorpio polarity. Scorpio is the objective aspect of learning to penetrate and utterly transform one's self, like the phoenix rising out of the ashes.*

*Where we find the Venus-Scorpio Pentagram may describe what we value in a marriage. For example in the 11th house we would want our married partner to also be a good friend. If a VPP is in the 2nd house we might wish to marry an artist.*

*Scorpio teaches us about involvement with others. Many intense Pluto lessons are faced as we recognize and end the misuse of power and align our sexuality to the divine. Ultimately as we learn to share, we find ourselves able to encourage others to self-empower.*

# Strength Rules Leo
*Excerpt from Leigh McCloskey*

Strength is the 8th Key in the Tarot Arcana and is represented astrologically by the fixed fire sign Leo. Leo is associated with the qualities of nobility, creative self-expression and power.

One of the titles attributed to the archetype of Strength is the path where fire becomes light, suggesting a transmutation wherein the fire of cosmic mind is transformed into the informing light of consciousness within manifestation.

The emphasis of Strength is that the personality or ego must develop sympathetic qualities necessary for these greater informing energies to function consciously. ☯

TAROT—STRENGTH—Key #8
One of 22 original pen and ink drawings by Leigh J McCloskey from his masterwork of original art & writing, "Tarot ReVisioned,"(Olandar Press 2003)

Find the Pentagram Point closest to your birth year, month and day. Place the current VPP into your natal chart. The house in which it is located will show you how the Venus-Sun-Earth Inferior or Superior Conjunction is working in your life. All five of the Pentagram points are attractors, and they will line up with important events and in the charts of those individuals with whom you share the journey of life. Venus's Pentagram Star Point in Leo correlates to your creative self expression and self actualization.

# THE LEO
## PENTAGRAM STAR DATES

| | |
|---|---|
| Aug 23 1987 | 29°Le36' D ES |
| Aug 22 1991 | 29°Le14' R |
| Aug 20 1995 | 27°Le29' D |
| Aug 20 1999 | 27°Le02' R |
| Aug 18 2003 | 25°Le23' D |
| Aug 17 2007 | 24°Le50' R |
| Aug 16 2011 | 23°Le17' D |
| Aug 15 2015 | 22°Le39' R |
| Aug 14 2019 | 21°Le11' D |
| Aug 13 2023 | 20°Le28' R |
| Aug 11 2027 | 19°Le06' D |
| Aug 10 2031 | 18°Le17' R |
| Aug 09 2035 | 17°Le01' D |
| Aug 08 2039 | 16°Le06' R |

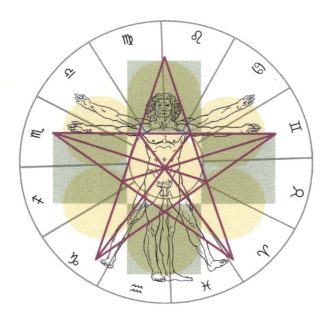

# THE LEO PENTAGRAM STAR

*Leo is one half of the Leo/Aquarius polarity. Leo is the subjective side. The Venus Pentagram point will show us by house placement where we need to express ourselves creatively and fully embrace joy, love and fun.*

*The position of the Venus Pentagram Star may point to where we value or find romantic love.*

*For example, if a Pentagram Point is in the 10th house we could meet a love interest in our workplace; in the 6th house at the gym; in the 3rd house at school etc..*

*Leo and Aquarius integrate through learning to be of service to the whole (Aq), and by using the unique talents of the self (Leo).*

## LOVERS RULES GEMINI
*Excerpt from Leigh McCloskey*

The Lovers is the 6th Key in the Tarot Arcana and is represented astrologically by the mutable air sign Gemini, the twin, which is associated with communication, duality, curiosity, creativity, and intellectual dexterity.

Gemini is ruled by Mercury, the planet attributed to the Magus. The Lovers, like the Magus, symbolize the potentiality for the inner or higher self to consciously mediate through the personality, liberating it to function as an unobstructed channel for the expression of transcendent mind.

...The Hebrew letter, Zain, meaning sword is attributed to the Lovers. The sword in tarot symbology corresponds with the element of air and is associated with the discriminatory powers of the mind.

The sword divides, separates, and penetrates. Its incisive function corresponds with reason, logic analysis, and informed choice. It suggests the intellect's ability to recognize intrinsic differences and interrelationships through contrast and comparison. ☯

**Nota Bene: EA teaches that Gemini names and classifies the physical world to make sense of Natural Law.**

TAROT—THE LOVERS—Key #6
One of 22 original pen and ink drawings by Leigh J McCloskey from his masterwork of original art & writing, "Tarot ReVisioned,"
(Olandar Press 2003)

Find the Pentagram Point closest to your birth year, month and day. Place the current VPP into your natal chart. The house in which it is located will show you how the Venus-Sun-Earth Inferior or Superior Conjunction is working in your life. All five of the Pentagram points are attractors, and they will line up with important events and in the charts of those individuals with whom you share the journey of life. Venus's Pentagram Star Point in Gemini correlates to your intellectual style and what you value knowing about most.

# THE GEMINI
## PENTAGRAM STAR DATES

| | |
|---|---|
| Jun 19 1964 | 28°Ge38' R MS |
| Jun 20 1968 | 29°Ge07' D |
| Jun 17 1972 | 26°Ge30' R |
| Jun 17 1976 | 27°Ge03' D |
| Jun 15 1980 | 2T4°Ge20' R |
| Jun 15 1984 | 24°Ge20' D |
| Jun 12 1988 | 22°Ge12' R |
| Jun 12 1992 | 22°Ge53' D |
| Jun 10 1996 | 20°Ge02' R |
| Jun 11 2000 | 20°Ge47' D |
| Jun 08 2004 | 17°Ge53' R |
| Jun 08 2008 | 18°Ge42' D |
| Jun 05 2012 | 15°Ge44' R |
| Jun 06 2016 | 16°Ge35' D |
| Jun 03 2020 | 13°Ge35' R |
| Jun 04 2024 | 14°Ge29' D |
| Jun 01 2028 | 11°Ge26' R |
| Jun 02 2032 | 12°Ge23' D |
| May 29 2036 | 09°Ge02' R |

# THE GEMINI PENTAGRAM STAR

**Gemini is one half of the Gemini/Sagittarius polarity. Gemini is the subjective side wherein we learn to name, categorize, classify and use logic to discern the order of the world we are navigating.**

**The polarity Sagittarius deals with Natural Law. So the style in which you communicate and learn, and the truth you are uncovering, will be aligned with the position of your Gemini Pentagram Star Point in your chart.**

**The cyclical unfolding of Gemini requires us to gather as much data as we can hold. Then new information arrives, creating a withdrawal and a movement back to the inner knowing of the Soul.**

# EMPEROR RULES ARIES

*Excerpt from Leigh McCloskey*

The Emperor is the 4th Key in the Tarot Arcana and is represented astrologically by the cardinal fire sign Aries. Aries is associated with self-awareness, pioneering spirit, courage, leadership, and intelligence.

The Emperor is the initiator, that which the Empress holds in potential, the Emperor ignites, sets into motion. He is the grand architect of the universe, also known as the ancient of days.

The Sun is exalted in Aries, suggesting that the Emperor represents the life-creating and sustaining fire or force which permeates and acts as creative impulse within all growth. Mars rules the astrological sign of Aries. ☯

TAROT—THE EMPEROR—Key #4
One of 22 original pen and ink drawings by Leigh J McCloskey from his masterwork of original art & writing, "Tarot ReVisioned,"
(Olandar Press 2003)

Find the Pentagram Point closest to your birth year, month and day. Place the current VPP into your natal chart. The house in which it is located will show you how the Venus-Sun-Earth Inferior or Superior Conjunction is working in your life. All five of the Pentagram points are attractors, and they will line up with important events and in the charts of those individuals with whom you share the journey of life. Venus's Pentagram Point in Aries correlates to your fierce desire to express yourself and is where you will need to find healthy ways to value your need to do your own thing.

# THE ARIES
## PENTAGRAM STAR DATES

| | |
|---|---|
| Apr 20 1929 | 29°Ar48' R MS |
| Apr 21 1933 | 01° Tau05' D |
| Apr 17 1937 | 27°Ar35' R |
| Apr 19 1941 | 28°Ar50' D |
| Apr 15 1945 | 25°Ar20' R |
| Apr 16 1949 | 26°Ar36' D |
| Apr 13 1953 | 23°Ar06' R |
| Apr 14 1957 | 24°Ar20' D |
| Apr 10 1961 | 20°Ar51' R |
| Apr 11 1965 | 22°Ar03' D |
| Apr 08 1969 | 18°Ar36' R |
| Apr 09 1973 | 19°Ar47' D |
| Apr 06 1977 | 16°Ar20' R |
| Apr 07 1981 | 17°Ar28' D |
| Apr 03 1985 | 14°Ar05' R |
| Apr 04 1989 | 15°Ar09' D |
| Apr 01 1993 | 11°Ar49' R |
| Apr 02 1997 | 12°Ar51' D |
| Mar 29 2001 | 09°Ar31' R |
| Mar 30 2005 | 10°Ar31' D |
| Mar 27 2009 | 07°Ar15' R |
| Mar 28 2013 | 08°Ar10' D |
| Mar 25 2017 | 04°Ar57' R |
| Mar 26 2021 | 05°Ar50' D |
| Mar 22 2025 | 02°Ar39' R |
| Mar 23 2029 | 03°Ar28' D |
| Mar 20 2033 | 00°Ar21' R |
| Mar 21 2037 | 01°Ar05' D * |

# THE ARIES PENTAGRAM STAR

*Aries is one half of the Aries/Libra polarity. Aries is the subjective side wherein the soul will push us to fulfill our desires, with self-honouring.*

*Aries and Libra have a strong intention to relate passionately with others. The VPP in Aries will enhance the desires that emanate from our soul. These desires must have freedom of expression, and the VPP in Aries causes us to really fight for our need to avoid all restrictions in pursuing our desires.*

*The Aries perpetual state of becoming requires us to spring into action. The World saw the Arab Spring arise with a VPP in Aries within weeks of the Planet Uranus also reentering Aries.*

*Nota Bene: Dates for Uranus in Aries are: 5/27/2010-8/13/2010 & 3/11/2011 to 5/16/2018 & 11/6/2018 to 3/7/2019.*

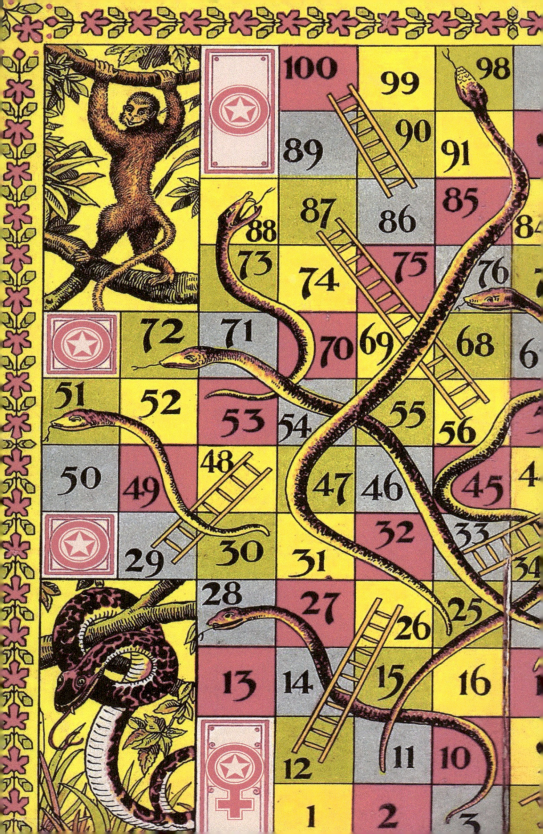

## Part Four:
### CYCLES, PHASES & STAGES

Use the workbook at the end of this book to plot the positions and the movement of Venus from Morning Star to Evening Star.

Access the links to the ephemerides to look up the movement of Venus around the time of your birth.

By studying the phase and gate of the Moon/Venus Descent or Ascent of your natal Venus phase at birth you will know more about where you are in this larger cycle of evolutionary momentum.

What kind of Kumari Kiss did you come to Earth to receive?

Those born in the 1960s came for the evolution/revolution.

Those born in the 1980s came for the Capricorn stellium which changed world order. ☯

# VENUS RETROGRADE

Venus Rx, with its Uranian flavor, will correlate to unusual relationships and experiences. Depending on the sign and phases, it is possible for Venus Rx to indicate changes in behavior that look like a sharp left turn. As we realign with Natural Law we should be able to observe a type of Snakes-&-Ladders in the Descent phase of Venus. This looks like people showing up who allow us to re experience unresolved relationship issues.

During Venus Rx, we are more likely to be able to break away from our consensus conditioning. Wherever we have suppressed our desires, the retrograde phenomenon then assists us to access the subconscious, and sort out the repressed contents.

JWG also taught about "the karmic/evolutionary requirement in order to become realigned with actual reality." Retrograde periods also help us realign with Natural Law. We need to stop projecting our limiting beliefs onto the existing reality, and during the Rx passage of Venus, it is easier to do so. When Venus is Rx we are reliving, repeating and redoing the unfinished business in key karmic relationships.

Conditions will be set up that will emphasize our own individuation. We are watching the release of traumas in regard to patriarchal domination/submission dynamics, martyrdom and masochism. Violation of the feminine—as the patriarchy grinds to a slow end—will be necessarily faced. ☯

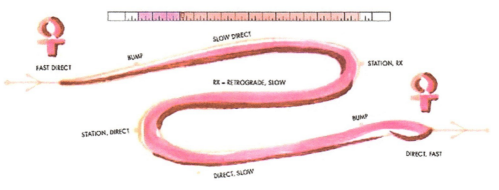

Venus Retrograde
Illustration by George Ozuna

**VENUS KEYWORDS**—Beauty, Sensory Pleasure, Music, Art, Money, Possessions, Income, Material Values

**INNER SIDE OF VENUS—TAURUS**—Relationship with Self

**OUTER SIDE OF VENUS—LIBRA**—Relationships with Others

**FEMININE PRINCIPLE**—Nature-Based, Interconnected Existence of all Creation, which is the Creative Vessel of Life that contains, Nurtures and Protects

**RELATIONSHIPS**—A Variety of Relationships (Marriage is Scorpio), Business Relationships, Partnerships and Counselee/Counselor Relationships

**COOPERATION**—Listening to the Other, Diplomacy, Agreements, Compromise and Alliance

**NATURAL LAW**—Sharing, Caring and Inclusion

**INTERACTION**—Socializing, Relating, Comparing, Evaluating, Give-and-Take, Reflection and Mirroring

# The Cycles Of Venus

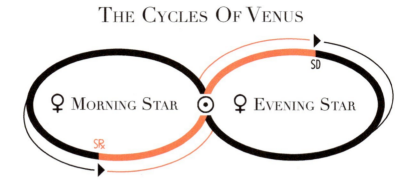

## VENUS MORNING STAR

Venus begins Her Retrograde after Maximum Brilliance and spends 40 days in total as she transitions from ES to MS.

## INFERIOR CONJUNCTION

...occurs when Venus is between the Earth and the Sun.

The first part of the Morning Star phase occurs while Venus is retrograde, and it is therefore a time of self-authentication. We must now disengage and let go of the values that no long serve our soul's growth. As Venus Rx is correlating to a time for individuation—this is when we may be more withdrawn from consensus values and those social mores to which others adapt so easily.

## A NEW VPP FORMS

...at the Inferior Conjunction. The mythic Kiss of the Kumari brings a gift of light from the fiery interaction of Venus and the Sun. It helps us with the Descent ahead, as we discover how to disengage and let go of the values that no long serve our soul's growth.

## VENUS MS DIRECT

The Descent of Venus occurs after Venus continues her direct motion, and she now meets the Moon seven times. Venus MS, direct, infused with Light is courageous and brave as she heads to Sunlight. She disappears and reappears as an Evening Star.

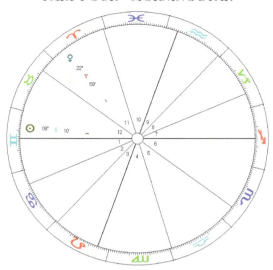

## THE SEVEN GATES

...represent the seven stages of growth wherein we release old values and gain insights into our emotional body correlating to the Venus—Moon conjunctions.

This is the gibbous phase of Venus. Forward evolutionary motion must match inner growth. Inner growth must align personal desire to soul desire.

During the Venus Morning Star Descent, we can search for our individual expression on many fronts, depending on the sign placement and other factors of Venus.

All efforts will be emboldened by the development of our personal self-worth.

## VENUS MS TRANSITS

The *Transit of Venus* MS Descent shows Venus slowly descending in the morning sky. The Snakes-&-Ladders tests begin.

We must be more introverted as we are releasing outworn modes of being throughout the seven new Venus-Moon conjunctions.

In order to internalize and differentiate our true self from the values and social mores of the consensus, we must use these Moon-Venus conjunctions to align ourselves authentically with Natural Law.

We have provided a work book that allows you to journal your self-discovery!

## THE CYCLES OF VENUS

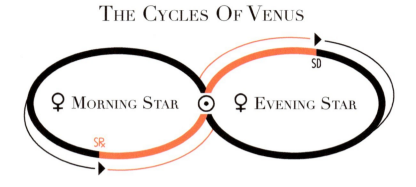

### VENUS ES IN SUNLIGHT

During the first several weeks of its Evening Star phase, the light of Venus is lost in solar glare. Metaphorically she is in the realm of her sister Ereshkigal and will soon begin her Ascent phase.

### SUPERIOR CONJUNCTION

The Venus-Earth Superior Conjunction occurs when Venus is behind the Sun. During the Venus ES phase, Venus is moving at or near maximum velocity.

### A NEW VPP FORMS

A VPP Star forms again at Superior Conjunction when Venus is direct and moving through the zodiac—near its maximum speed. Once again, when the

Sun and Venus meet at the same degree of the zodiac and form a conjunction, we receive another Kumari Kiss.

This occurs in the Full Phase of the 584 day Venus Cycle, thus compelling us to complete social tasks and work on how we relate more objectively to the world and others.

### VENUS EVENING STAR

Venus rises as an Evening Star, and a few weeks after the Sun and Venus meet in a Superior Conjunction. Venus emerges on the other side of the Sun, appearing as the Evening Star.

### THE SEVEN GATES

At each of the Venus ES gates, we integrate values and insights

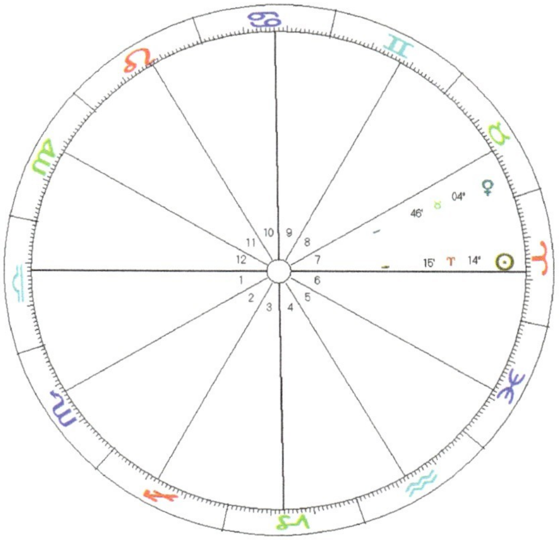


into our emotional body, correlating to the Venus-Moon conjunctions.

The ES Seven Gates correlate to the Balsamic Phase. The events and experiences of the past year's descent cycle has given us a wider perspective as we choose the path forward.

Evening Star periods are social in nature due to the opposition of Venus and the Sun and thus they may feel like a more deliberate and goal-oriented period.

The events and experiences of the past year's descent cycle has given us a wider perspective as we choose the path forward.

The Ascent of the seven Venus-Moon conjunctions correlates eventually to the reward and the return with the elixir in Joseph Campbell's Monomyth. See the Monomyth table.

## VENUS ES RX

Venus ES spends 40 days in RX motion just before the Inferior Conjunction. She switches from ES to MS during that time.

## TRANSITS

During the ES Ascent Direct, we are likely to be extroverted. It is a time of building relationships throughout the seven new Ascent Venus-Moon conjunctions of the balsamic phase.

Those who are successful in finding their authentic voice are often influencers if that is within their soul's purpose. ☯

# Venus Morning Star

In an ancient Sumerian myth, The Myth of Inanna, the visible and invisible passage of Venus is told as a story of the Goddess Inanna, who was also aligned with Venus and called the Queen of Heaven.

We are told of her journey as she descends to attend the funeral of her sister's husband. Her sister rules as the Queen of the Underworld.

As Inanna begins her passage, she must purify herself to enter the sister's realm. She does this by leaving a piece of jewelry or clothing at each of the Seven Gates, which are aligned to the seven chakras.

These Seven Gates correlate to seven Venus-Moon Conjunctions, as Venus shifts from a Rx Morning star to a SD Evening Star.

At each of the Seven Gates Inanna passes, as she moves towards the Superior Conjunction, Inanna must release attachments to all of her belongings.

She finally arrives in the other world absolutely naked/innocent and is killed by her sister. ☯

Based on the Burney Babylon 1800-1750 Relief

Based on the Burney Babylon 1800-1750 Relief

# Venus Evening Star

Venus begins her Ascent after she forms a new Pentagram Point and appears as an Evening Star.

She ascends backup through the Seven Gates where she is restored by putting back on the objects she had removed on her Descent.

I have provided a table of these dates to help you observe and correlate these Seven Gates with the Ascent of Venus.

The Ascent is a period of personal empowerment.

See the tables which correlate Venus to Joseph Campbell's Monomyth.

Use the tables of the Seven Gates. We offer keywords to help you with your own self-empowering passage. ☯

## PART FIVE:
### EVOLUTIONARY STAGES

The information on the stages will help you understand the unfolding of Natural Law.

Jeffrey Wolf Green has given us a model to help us move through codependency, independence and interdependence.

These psychological models are called consensus, individuation and spirituality in the EA Paradigm.

Practice orienting yourself as a soul on an evolutionary journey.

The phases and stages are aspects of Natural Law.

It is a vast study, and these parts of the puzzle are very helpful to orient yourself on evolutionary journey. ☯

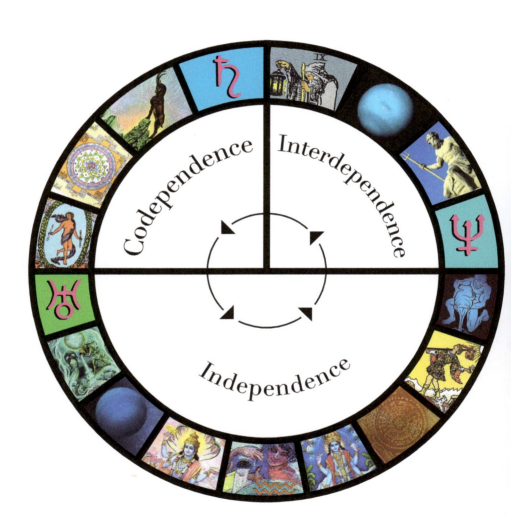

For more information:

http://schoolofevolutionaryastrology.com/our-store
https://www.youtube.com/user/SongsLinda/videos
https://rosemarcus.com/
http://kristinfontana.com/

# The Stages Of Evolutionary Growth

| Stage 1 | | | Stage 2 | | | Stage 3 | | |
|---|---|---|---|---|---|---|---|---|
| CODEPENDENCY | | | INDEPENDENCE | | | INTERDEPENDENCE | | |
| ♄ SATURN Consensus | | | ♅ URANUS Individuated | | | ♆ NEPTUNE Spiritual | | |
| Saturn | Uranus | Neptune | Saturn | Uranus | Neptune | Saturn | Uranus | Neptune |
| Consensus /consensus | Consensus /individuating | Consensus /spiritual | Individuating /consensus | Individuating /individuating | Individuating /spiritual | Spiritual /consensus | Spiritual /individuating | Spiritual /spiritual |

# Stage 1

## CODEPENDENCE

The Saturn informed consensus stage of evolution correlates to conformity at all costs. In this stage we don't question the existing rules, we accept the dogma; we crave acceptance and wish to fit in.

## SATURN—CONSENSUS

Consensus is a psychological condition of codependency. We wish to be attached at the hip to others who share our need to fit in.

## URANUS—CONSENSUS

We are still in herd mentality mode, but we would like to try out our own talents and ideas, and fulfill some unique desires, without losing the approval of others.

## NEPTUNE—CONSENSUS

In the Neptune stage of codependence, we might choose to be the band leader, or the Maestro or Choir leader of the church. We care more about the collective and will act in the way that shows we need our connection to the group.

# Stage 2

## INDEPENDENCE

Uranus informs the stage of Independence. As we move through the Independent stages, we are seeking to Individuate. To find our unique expression, we will generally need to rebel from the consensus. JWG called this "Freedom from the Known."

In this stage we stop copying others, and although we don't give a hoot, others may now wish to copy us.

## SATURN—INDIVIDUATED

I like to joke that these are the folks at the Star Wars Conventions. We have chosen our unique mask, but are still a card-carrying member of the group.

Although we want to be a part of a group, we are ready to explore what makes us unique. We generally must individuate with others, or identify with those also searching for their unique self-expression.

Because Saturn is involved with Uranus, we are attempting to make unique copies, instead of just copying others wholesale.

## URANUS—INDIVIDUATED

These are the rock stars and the Picasso's of our world, doing their own thing, and often getting a lot of attention for doing so.

This is the arena of the most individuation, so we have placed a lot of attention on these souls. They often become the example of what is possible if you really get good at doing your own thing.

## NEPTUNE—INDIVIDUATED

Here we find Steve Jobs and the presidents and members of the tech revolution, who are making a better world for us all with unique inventions. The corporate world, film makers—basically our mechanical level of life—exists here and these are the souls interested in dreaming (Neptune) up a better world (Saturn).

# STAGE 3
## INTERDEPENDENCE

Neptune informs the stages of Interdependence. As we move through the Interdependent stages, we are learning about Natural Law and how we project our beliefs onto the existing reality.

## SATURN—SPIRITUAL

I love to comment about the shadow consensus of the New Age—group hugs, group mind, wearing all orange, and health food crazes. We are in a consensus mode in the first level of this stage, and so of course we are learning to navigate domination/submission paradigms. They are Neptune in nature so here comes the Gurus.

## URANUS—SPIRITUAL

Eventually we learn how to be self-empowered. We want to find our own unique way. Here we interact with Natural Law above all else. We often become a leader of Neptunian-type movements. The challenge with this stage is forgetting that Uranus is about using your gift(s) for the collective greater good. The way through it is to keep humble and to keep high and wide. Align the heart with a love for humanity and do good deeds.

## NEPTUNE—SPIRITUAL

So becoming the Master of Two Worlds is the outcome of this journey. Realization of Natural Law and keeping yourself available to serve humanity is another.

The point of our life on earth is to fulfill our evolutionary intentions. Carrying out these intentions in this third stage has been linked throughout the Piscean Age with sacrifice. Gandhi, Mother Teresa, Jesus, Buddha, etc.. As we move towards the Aquarian Age sacrifice will fade as the keyword of the Kali Yuga.

What replaces it? Love for humanity. Absolute and complete alignment with your soul. A palpable experience of the Divine. Sharing. Caring. Inclusion. ☯

Stages of Evolutionary Growth Chart
Designed & Illustration by George Ozuna

# MODERNIZING THE MYTH
## THE DESCENT OF THE GODDESS

In its broadest outline, Joseph Campbell's Monomyth or Hero's Journey, takes the form of a descent into and return from something other
than the known. Whether real or metaphorical, it is a descent into an
underworld followed by a miraculous return.

Joseph Campbell states that this Journey involves three stages: "a
separation from the world, a penetration into some source of power,
and a life-enhancing return."

A modern description in Evolutionary Astrological terms describes a
separation from a consensus community and a disorienting rite of passage, where one is faced with tests of self-empowerment. This leads
to a reintegration with the community, having attained a true identity
aligned with innate Natural Law.

In Evolutionary Astrology we correlate this to outgrowing consensus
mentality, individuating and then finding one's interdependence within
society.

**Carl Jung: "One does not become enlightened by figures of light,
but by imagining making the darkness conscious."**

The myth of Inanna and Ereshkigal are allegorical stories of the passage of Venus as she shifts from Morning Star to Evening Star. Inanna
and Ereshkigal—the light and dark sides of the goddess—are insepa-
rable aspects of the alchemical process of the transformation of the
soul. ☯

# MODERNIZING THE HERO'S MYTH

Modernizing the Hero's Monomyth Chart
Designed & Illustration by George Ozuna

## 1. ORDINARY WORLD—00°
Our story begins here in our current evolutionary condition wherein we experience a lack.

## 2. CALL TO ADVENTURE—30°
Dissatisfaction happens sometimes around an eclipse, a gateway, a pentagram star, a retrograde—something opens us up.

## 3. REFUSAL OF THE CALL—45°
Resistance, Reluctance, Denial, Fear. Not wanting to step out of our comfort zone.

## 4. MEETING THE MENTOR—72°
The hero meets a reflection/person or spiritual guide that can ready her or him for the journey ahead.

## 5. CROSSING THE THRESHOLD—102.5°
The hero goes on the adventure seeking to fulfill inherent potentials and intending to go forward.

## 6. TEST ALLIES ENEMIES—135°
Strategic alliances are made and resistances are progressively encountered, so that the hero can resolve his inner conflicts, and continue to individuate from external conditioning.

## 7. ORDEAL—150°
Hurdles, obstacles and flying monkeys are unleashed as the hero's journey correlates to just how he/she might be calling forth a crisis, to accelerate his or her evolution.

## 8. MEETING WITH THE GODDESS—180°
The feminine wisdom becomes a guide towards unconditional or perfect love and wholeness.

## 9. TEMPTATION—206°
Our Integrity, Authenticity, Responsibility, Sharing, Caring and Inclusion are tested. Redo, Renew, Review, Recapitulate to proceed.

## 10. ATONEMENT W/ AUTHORITY—216°
The hero must confront all domination/submission paradigms by seeing what holds the ultimate outer power. And then take back the projected illusion as his or her journey of self-empowerment continues.

## 11. APOTHEOSIS—225°
Transformation happens because realization garnered from Natural Law moves the hero onto higher ground. Acting beyond doubt and fear, he/she finds divine alignment with God/dess, Source—All that is.

## 12. REWARD—240°
Having exhausted many separating desires the hero may now receive the rewards/talents that enhance self-empowerment.

## 13. REFUSING TO RETURN—270°
The hero can get stuck emotionally with a trine-like scenario and hesitate before acknowledging the divine, which he/she is now asked to serve.

## 14. MAGICAL FLIGHT—300°
Having realized the path involves helping others, the hero makes a commitment to find new ways to share the rewards.

## 15. RESCUE FROM WITHOUT—320°
The interdependent God/dess intervenes to assist the hero choosing forward evolutionary movement.

## 16. THE ROAD BACK—330°
Elimination of all separating desires, the hero only wishes to be reunited with the cause of creation, God/dess, Source, all that is. The hero embodies Natural Law.

## 17. MASTER OF TWO WORLDS—360°
Surrender to the journey of life. Mastery is demonstrated by the hero's ability to be in the flow with the universe, aligned with God/dess, all that is. ☙

THE 17 STAGES OF JOSEPH CAMBELL'S MONOMYTH

Codependence

Independence

YANG
NEW PHASE

YIN
CRESCENT PHASE

YANG
FIRST QUARTER PHASE

YIN
GIBBOUS PHASE

0°
30°
40°
45°
51°
60°
72°
90°
102.5°
120°
135°
150°

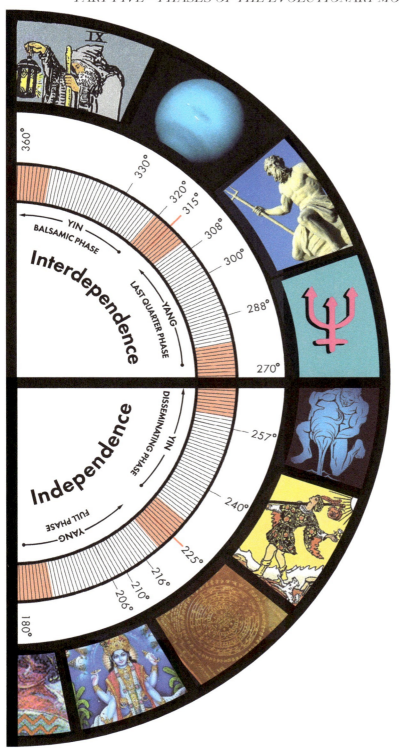

YIN
BALSAMIC PHASE

LAST QUARTER PHASE

YANG

**Interdependence**

DISSEMINATING PHASE

YIN

**Independence**

FULL PHASE

YANG

360°
330°
320°
315°
308°
300°
288°
270°
257°
240°
225°
216°
210°
206°
180°

### 0°-45° New Phase-A New Evolutionary Intention Is Seeded

**CONJUNCTION AT** 0°
***Ordinary World*-**Self Discovery, New Beginning

SEMI-SEXTILE AT 30°
***Call To Adventure*-**Narrowing of Focus, Direction

NOVILE AT 40°
*Desire Is Triggered*, Awareness of One's Personal Involvement

SEMI-SQUARE AT 45°
Conflict As Desire For More Emerges


### 45°-90° Crescent Phase-Internalizing The Process

**SEMI-SQUARE AT** 45°
***Refusal of the Call*-**First crisis that it will take a focus of energy

SEPTILE AT 51°
Special Identity, Aspect of fated interactions to keep the soul on track

SEXTILE AT 60°
Opportunity for growth, action is externalized

QUINTILE AT 72°
***Meeting The Mentor*-**Creative transformation. Meaning becomes highly internalized, receives a map or information

SQUARE AT 90°
Compression, An unconscious fear of failure. A push/pull

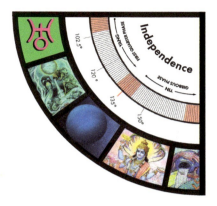

## 90°-135° First Quarter Phase-Crisis in Action

### CONJUNCTION AT 90°
The need to initiate actions or forms before you can move forward

BI-SEPTILE AT 102.5°
*Crossing The First Threshold*

TRINE AT 120°
Creating a foundation, Creative actualization

SESQUIQUADRATE AT 135°
Narcissus/Humility, The soul has a newly realized intent.

## 135°-180° Gibbous-Humility To Serve Social Order

### SESQUIQUADRATE AT 135°
*Tests, Allies Enemies*-Hero must now analyze and adjust strategies

BI-QUNITILE AT 144°
Service to the whole, Using ones special capacity

INCONJUNCT AT 150°
*Ordeal*-Adjustments, Clarification or confusion

TRI-SEPTILE AT 154°
Loss of self-delusion reveals purpose to the collective social order

OPPOSITION AT 180°
Equality. As opposition forces oneself to improve their social skills

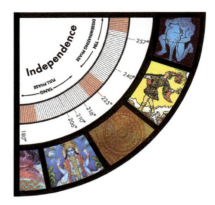

## 180°-225° New Phase-Social Immersion/ Social Withdrawal

**OPPOSITION AT** 180°
***Meeting With The Goddess***-Integration of self and society progresses

TRI-SEPTILE AT 206°
***Temptation***-Cooperation with social order, Relativity must be realized

INCONJUNCT AT 210°
Adjustments to personal and social limitations. Humility or humiliation

BI-QUNITILE AT 216°
***Atonement With Outer Authority***-Serving the collective, refining
special skills

SESQUIQUADRATE AT 225°
Getting schooling, credentials & skills

## 225°-270° Disseminating-Social obligation/ Service

**SESQUIQUADRATE AT** 225°
***Apotheosis***-New input & new visions-getting it together to fit into the social
order to serve it.

TRINE AT 240°
***Reward***-Presentation of the talented individual is well received

BI-SEPTILE AT 257°
Integrate, establish, actualize, disseminate, mastering the complexity of social
interaction.

SQUARE AT 270°
Rebellion against the collective thought forms emerge as larger ideas evolve.

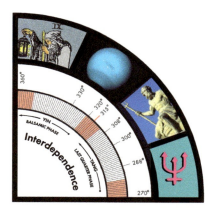

## 270°-315° Last Quarter Phase-Crisis in Consciousness

### SQUARE AT 270°

***Refusing To Return***-Deconditioning of the collective consensus must begin.

### QUNITILE AT 288°

An increasing understanding of Natural Law.

### SEXTILE AT 300°

***Magical Flight***-Light Workers, The ability to flow with a higher purpose, or extreme stuckness

### SEPTILE AT 308°

Refinement

### SEMI-SQUARE AT 315°

Internalized stress to withdraw from collective consensus of any kind.

## 315°-360° Balsamic Phase-Completion

### SEMI SQUARE AT 315°

The conflict to withdraw versus the need to fulfill material obligations must be achieved by doing both.

### NOVILE AT 320°

***Rescue From Without***-Ready to jump. The Fool

### SEMI-SEXTILE AT 330°

***The Road Back***-allow new patterns to guide the self to its place in the larger social context or universal order.

### CONJUNCTION AT 360°

***Master of Two Worlds***-Evolutionary Completion. 🌑

# Part Six:
# How To Use The Workbook

For your convenience we have provided an example of how the workbook looks when filled in with the Venus Pentagram Points, Planets, Asteroids, Ascendant, Descendant, MC and IC, as well as the Lunar Nodes.

The closest VPP to your birth is your VPP#1. Make sure that the VPP#1 is in the same phase—Evening Star or Morning Star—as your Natal Venus.

The links will guide you to ephemerides that give the positions of the VPP. You can also verify whether Venus is a Morning Star or Evening Star using the links provided below.

We also offer the Vitruvian Wheel to superimpose onto your Natal Chart if you wish to do so.

There are useful Workbook pages to interact with the Monomyth, EA Phases, Aspects and Chakras. Compare your chart to the Seven Gates, and both the transiting and Natal VPPs. This will help you understand the unfolding Natural Law.☯

http://aastl.net/FindYourVenusStarPoint.pdf
https://www.astro.com/swisseph/ae/venus1600.pdf

# Workbook

## Venus Through the Signs

|  | Extrovert | Introvert | Desire |
|---|---|---|---|
| ♈ | Fearless, Adventurer Explorer High Energy Fun | Independence, Loner, Warrior | Separation |
| ♉ | Sensual Pleasure Oriented Earthy Real | Artist, Patient, Materialistic | Self-sufficiency |
| ♊ | Playful, Smart, Curious, Loves Dichotomy, Needs Fun | Bookworm, Taking A Class, Teaching A Class | Naming |
| ♋ | Nurturing, Cozy, Witches, Parenting | Cooking, Home Body, Security Conscious | Security |
| ♌ | Party Animal, Creative, Sweet As Honey | Romantic, Purposeful, Strong | Creativity |
| ♍ | Musically Gifted, Researcher, Good Listeners | Service, Self-improvement, Discernment | Improvement |

| | | | |
|---|---|---|---|
| ♈ Aries | ♋ Cancer | ♎ Libra | ♑ Capricorn |
| ♉ Taurus | ♌ Leo | ♏ Scorpio | ♒ Aquarius |
| ♊ Gemini | ♍ Virgo | ♐ Sagittarius | ♓ Pisces |

*Venus correlates with both our inner relationship to ourselves, and also relationships with others; Venus—Taurus and Venus— Libra. In this fun graph I have made some light keywords for the introverted and extroverted aspects of Venus. Enjoy!* ☯

|  | **Extrovert** | **Introvert** | **Desire** |
|---|---|---|---|
| ♎ | Dating, Good At Relating | Listening, Pleasing, Graceful | Relationship |
| ♏ | Tantric Initiate In Training | Sensual, Intimate, Marrying | Commitment |
| ♐ | Traveler, Philosopher, Lifetime Student, Funny | Wise, Truthful, Explorer | Natural Law |
| ♑ | Leader Of The Pack, Dependable, Strong, Truthful, Dignified | Conformist, Traditional, Responsible | Maturity |
| ♒ | Inventors, Social Animal, Best Friend, Insanely Fun | Individuating, Rebellious, Telepathic | Liberation |
| ♓ | Honey Pie Itself, Kind, Contemplative, Soulful, Musical | Poet, Dreamer, Faithful | GOD |

Here is an example of the Workbook page plotted with the Venus Pentagram Points, Planets, Asteroids and other Celestial Positions from a natal horoscope.

| Name: George | | Phase: Evening Star |
|---|---|---|
| POINTS | DEGREE | ZODIAC SIGN |
| 1 VPP | 01° | VIRGO |
| 2 VPP | 24° | GEMINI ℞ |
| 3 VPP | 17° | ARIES |
| 4 VPP | 01° | AQUARIUS ℞ |
| 5 VPP | 11° | SCORPIO |
| | | |
| SUN | 04° | PISCES |
| MOON | 11° | GEMINI |
| VENUS | 16° | ARIES |
| MERCURY | 21° | PISCES |
| MARS | 06° | VIRGO ℞ |
| JUPITER | 05° | VIRGO ℞ |
| SATURN | 25° | VIRGO ℞ |
| | | |
| URANUS | 25° | SCORPIO |
| NEPTUNE | 22° | SAGITTARIUS |
| PLUTO | 21° | LIBRA ℞ |
| | | |
| NO NODE | 29° | LEO ℞ |
| SO NODE | 29° | AQUARIUS ℞ |
| M.C. | 24° | SAGITTARIUS |
| I.C. | 24° | GEMINI |
| ASC | 21° | PISCES |
| CHIRON | 09° | TAURUS |
| CERES | 24° | ARIES |
| PALLAS | 14° | PISCES |
| JUNO | 16° | CANCER |
| ERIS | 14° | ARIES |
| VERTEX | 26° | VIRGO |
| LILLTH | 1° | VIRGO |

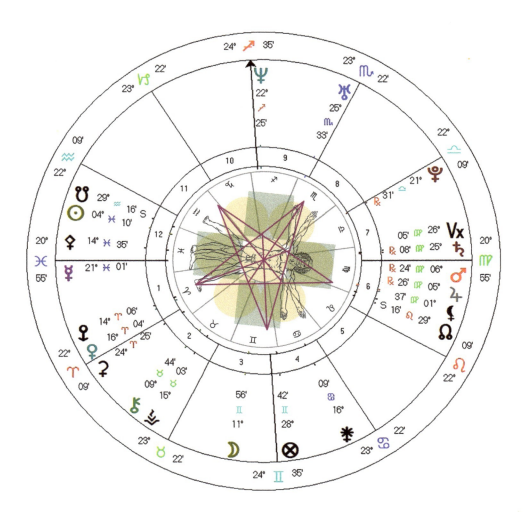

## CHOOSING YOUR VPP 1

Prior to Birth there was a Superior Conjunction
Aug 25 1979 at 1° VIRGO 43'21 D

The Evening Star phase lasted until Jun 08 1980
so this is the correct "VPP1" for this chart, because
the person was born in the winter of 1980.

### *You can verify the Evening Star Phase here:*

https://www.astro.com/swisseph/ae/venus1600.pdf

| Name: George | Phase: Evening Star |
|---|---|
| **Points** | **Degree & Sign** |
| VPP 1 | 01° VIRGO |
| VPP 2 | 24° GEMINI ℞ |
| VPP 3 | 17° ARIES |
| VPP 4 | 01° AQUARIUS ℞ |
| VPP 5 | 11° SCORPIO |
| | |
| SUN | 04° PISCES |
| MOON | 11° GEMINI |
| VENUS | 16° ARIES |
| MERCURY | 21° PISCES |
| MARS | 06° VIRGO ℞ |
| JUPITER | 05° VIRGO ℞ |
| SATURN | 25° VIRGO ℞ |
| | |
| URANUS | 25° SCORPIO |
| NEPTUNE | 22° SAGITTARIUS |
| PLUTO | 21° LIBRA ℞ |
| | |
| NO NODE | 29° LEO ℞ |
| SO NODE | 29° AQUARIUS ℞ |
| M.C. | 24° SAGITTARIUS |
| I.C. | 24° GEMINI |
| ASC | 21° PISCES |
| CHIRON | 09° TAURUS |
| CERES | 24° ARIES |
| PALLAS | 14° PISCES |
| JUNO | 16° CANCER |
| ERIS | 14° ARIES |
| VERTEX | 26° VIRGO |
| VESTA | 15° TAURUS |
| LILLITH | 1° VIRGO |

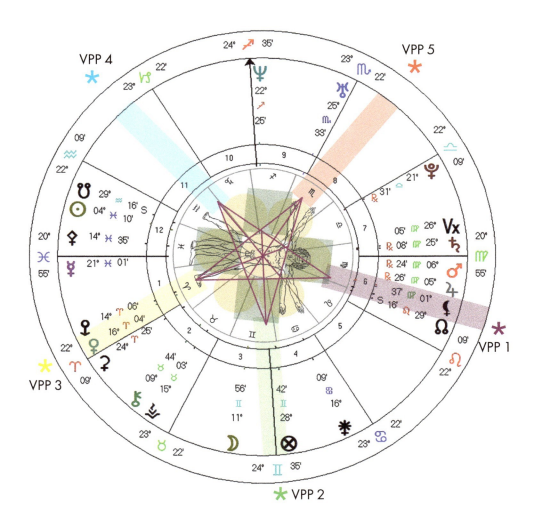

## PLOTTING KUMARI KISSES

Here we see how the VPP overlays onto a natal chart.

We also have all the Planets, Asteroids, Angles and Nodes in the grids.

Use the grids to correlate where the transiting VPP and the Seven Gates might be giving Kumari Kisses. ☯

| Name: | Phase: |
|---|---|
| **Points** | **Degree & Sign** |
| VPP 1 | |
| VPP 2 | |
| VPP 3 | |
| VPP 4 | |
| VPP 5 | |
| | |
| SUN | |
| MOON | |
| VENUS | |
| MERCURY | |
| MARS | |
| JUPITER | |
| SATURN | |
| | |
| URANUS | |
| NEPTUNE | |
| PLUTO | |
| | |
| NO NODE | |
| SO NODE | |
| M.C. | |
| I.C. | |
| ASC | |
| CHIRON | |
| CERES | |
| PALLAS | |
| JUNO | |
| ERIS | |
| VERTEX | |
| VESTA | |
| LILLITH | |

Use this blank wheel to fill in your positions or replace it with an online chart from astro.com

You can also superimpose the Vitruvian Wheel onto this chart. See example next page.

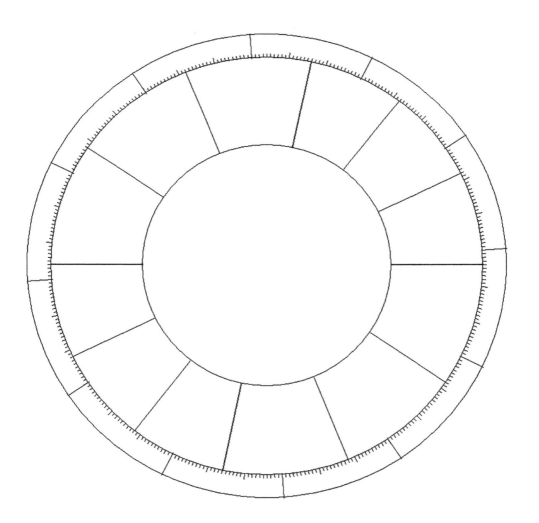

# VITRUVIAN WHEELS

Overlay the correct head star on your chart to see how the VPP interacts with your chart.

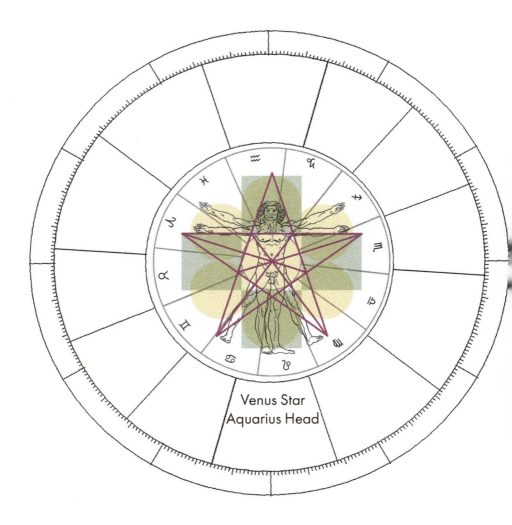

Venus Star
Aquarius Head

These five points inform astrologers about the people, resources, loves, values and relationships that each position of the (VPP) may signify by sign, aspect, phase and house position. ☯

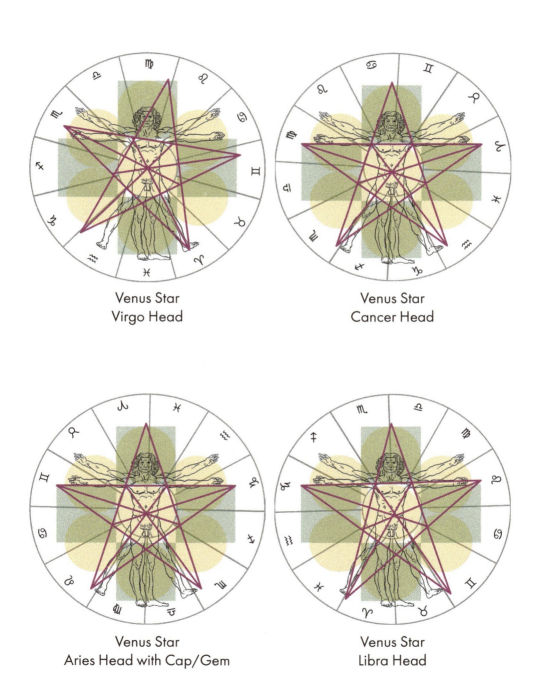

Venus Star
Virgo Head

Venus Star
Cancer Head

Venus Star
Aries Head with Cap/Gem

Venus Star
Libra Head

## Part Seven:
## 2017 Workbook

Here are the tables for 2017 for the Descent of Venus as She transitions from Morning Star to Evening Star.

These specific tables which we have provided assist in allowing you to go back and capture all your experiences as Venus moves through the Seven Gates of the Gibbous, Morning Star Phase.

These EA Keywords are given to help you with the Natural Law behind the movement of the Moon and Venus. Their Zodiacal positions for 2017 are offered here to study and to find patterns, especially if the degrees of the transits hit a Natal or Progressed Planet within a small orb of up to 3 degrees for Venus and the Moon.

We encourage you to take a few years to study this phenomenon. If you are working with others, you will be able to assist them to delve deeper into Natural Law inquiries. ☯

## 2017 MORNING STAR—Descent of Venus

**1st GATE—EA KEYWORDS PISCES—**"God Permeates All Consciousness."

As we are learning to overcome victim/martyrdom, and if we compliment more and complain less, we are more likely to see the perfection of creation. Pisces correlates to the desire to embrace God Consciousness wherein you recognize your interdependence.

**2nd GATE—EA KEYWORDS ARIES—**"Observe Separating Desires."

To connect with the evolutionary steps forward, we must honour the core need to be free to follow our instincts. Of course, balancing independence with consideration for others ensures we make progress now. This is a time to be centered, so that we can connect to the desires that help us with our lessons of equality consciousness.

**3rd GATE—EA KEYWORDS TAURUS—**"Self-Reliance & Self-Sufficiency."

Make sure to balance the need for self-sufficiency with a need to be happy in relationships. Spring is in the air and so we may be feeling frisky. Look around to see what is of value and consider what is needed to be more internally centered at this junction. Forward motion involves aligning with our higher values.

**4th GATE—EA KEYWORDS GEMINI—**"Classify, Identify &

Categorise."

The 27th degree of Gem/Sag correlates to the Galactic Center in our Milky Way, and to where our galaxy is headed in space. This sensitive degree helps us align with Natural Law. I recommend a course of study—a time of interaction with Nature. Naming the aspects of Natural Law is Gemini's gift. The Sagittarius polarity point invites us to embrace our Daemon Soul.

**5th GATE—EA KEYWORDS FOR CANCER—**"Identify Yourself As The Cause of Your Ego."

If the sign Cancer is highlighted and the Moon energies cause us to seek security from the outside, the lesson will be that security is actually only found within. Working on your relationship to Natural Law—is how you can make evolutionary steps forward now.

**6th GATE—EA KEYWORDS FOR LEO—**"Self-Actualizing Our Purpose."

As the summer solstice is also on the horizon, this juncture brings the Leonean desire for creative self-expression to the fore. It is an ideal time to balance our need for the Aquarius polarity of social integration. Avoiding the potential for narcissism, and instead using the strength of Leo's personal will to focus on our talent to connect to socially relevant themes, allows us to move forward now.

**7th GATE—EA KEYWORDS FOR LIBRA—**"Objective Consciousness."

Libra is a time when a shift from subjective to objective consciousness takes place. As we embrace our social needs, on a New Moon/Venus, it is quite likely we will attract new relationships. We must learn to listen to others now. Some of the issues that might come up: Are we on a two-way street? Are we attentive to the balance of self-honouring and responding to the needs of others? ☯

# SEVEN GATES-DESCENT OF VENUS 2017
## VENUS MOON CONJUNCTIONS

| New Pentagram | 03/25/2017 | 04° AR | Sun-Venus Inferior CNJ |
|---|---|---|---|
| Morning Star | 03/29/2017 | 02°AR | Heliacal Rise |
| | | | Moon Venus conjunctions |
| *Descent* | | | *NOTES* |
| Gate 1 | 04/23/2017 | 28°PIS | |
| Gate 2 | 05/22/2017 | 16°AR | |
| Gate 3 | 06/20/2017 | 14°TAU | |
| Gate 4 | 07/20/2017 | 17°GEM | |
| Gate 5 | 08/18/2017 | 21°CAN | |
| Gate 6 | 09/17/2017 | 27°LEO | |
| Gate 7 | 10/17/2017 | 4°LIB | |

# Seven Gates-Descent of Venus 2017

| 02/29/17 | Descent | Heliacal Rise of Venus | Morning Star |
|----------|---------|------------------------|--------------|
| | Moon Venus conjunctions | **JOSEPH CAMPBELL'S MONOMYTH** | |
| Gate 1 | 04/23/17 | Call to adventure-narrowing of focus-direction | 28° PIS |
| Gate 2 | 05/22/17 | Conflict as desire for more emerges | 16° AR |
| Gate 3 | 06/20/17 | Opportunity for growth, action is externalized | 14° TAU |
| Gate 4 | 07/20/17 | Meeting the mentor, creative transformation. Receives a map or information | 17° GEM |
| Gate 5 | 08/18/17 | The need to initiate actions or forms before you can move forward | 21° CAN |
| Gate 6 | 09/17/17 | Humility. The soul has a newly realized intention and must now analyze and adjust strategies | 27° LEO |
| Gate 7 | 10/17/17 | Equality. As opposition to one's ideas force oneself to face the others | 4° LIB |

# DESCENT OF VENUS
## PHASES OF VENUS 2017

| | | | |
|---|---|---|---|
| RETROGRADE | 03/04/17 | 13°♈08'R | VENUS RETROGRADE |
| EVENING SET | 03/22/17 | 07°♈00'R | RETROGRADE |
| HELIACAL RISE E | 03/29/17 | 02°♈34'R | MORNING STAR |
| DIRECT | 04/15/17 | 26°♓54' | VENUS DIRECT |
| GREATEST BRILLIANCE | 04/26/17 | 29°♓15' | FAST |
| GREATEST ELONGATION | 05/03/17 | 27°♈13' | FAST |
| SEVEN GATES | APR-OCT | 28°♓-04°♎ | SEE NEXT TABLE |
| MORNING SET | 11/28/17 | 26°♏54' | SOLAR GLARE |
| SUPERIOR CONJUNCTION | 01/08/18 | 18°♑57' | NEW PENTAGRAM |
| EVENING STAR | 02/18/18 | 10°♓42'D | EVENING STAR |

| | | | |
|---|---|---|---|
| ♈ Aries | ♋ Cancer | ♎ Libra | ♑ Capricorn |
| ♉ Taurus | ♌ Leo | ♏ Scorpio | ♒ Aquarius |
| ♊ Gemini | ♍ Virgo | ♐ Sagittarius | ♓ Pisces |

# Seven Gates-Descent of Venus 2017
## Descent of Morning Star

| DESCENT OF VENUS FROM MORNING STAR TO DISAPPEARANCE | | | |
|---|---|---|---|
| | 03/29/17 | Venus reappears as a Morning Star | 2° Aries |
| GATE 1 | 04/23/17 | **Seventh Chakra: Humility and Vastness** Transcendence. The Tenth Gate. The seat of the soul. Location: Soft spot on the crown of the head. | Inanna removes her crown 28° Pisces |
| GATE 2 | 05/22/17 | **Sixth Chakra: Intuition, Wisdom, Identity** The union of opposites; understanding one's purpose. Location: Eyebrow between eyes, thus the 3rd Eye. | Inanna gives her lapis lazuli staff 16° Aries |
| GATE 3 | 06/20/17 | **Fifth Chakra: Projective Power of the Word** Hearing and speaking the Truth. The Teacher. Location: Throat | Inanna removes the necklace from her throat 14° Taurus |
| GATE 4 | 07/20/17 | **Fourth Chakra: Heart: Love and Compassion** Awakening to spiritual awareness; forgiveness and service. Location: Chest/Heart. | Inanna takes of her chest plate 17° Gemini |
| GATE 5 | 08/18/17 | **Third Chakra: Solar Plexus: Action and Balance** Willpower. Personal power and commitment. Location: Navel, Solar Plexus. | Inanna removes a ring of power 21° Cancer |
| GATE 6 | 09/17/17 | **Second Chakra: Creativity** To feel, to desire, to create. Location: Sex Organs. | Inanna removes her golden hip girdle 27° Leo |
| GATE 7 | 10/17/17 | **First Chakra: Security and Survival** Foundation, survival, security, habit, self-acceptance. Location: End of the spine. | Inanna removes her royal breech-cloth 04° Libra |

## PART EIGHT:
## 2018 WORKBOOK

Here are the tables for 2018 for the Ascent of Venus as she transitions from Evening Star to Morning Star.

These specific tables which we have provided assist in allowing you to journal your experiences as Venus moves through the Seven Gates of the Balsamic, Evening Star Phase.

These EA Keywords are given to help you with the Natural Law behind the movement of the Moon and Venus. Their Zodiacal positions for 2018 can be studied, along with other years, to find patterns, especially if the degrees of the transits hit a Natal or Progressed Planet within a small orb of up to 3 degrees for Venus and the Moon.

We encourage you to take a few years to study this phenomenon. If you are working with others, you will be able to assist them to delve deeper into Natural Law inquiries. ☯

# 2018 EVENING STAR—Ascent of Venus

**1st GATE—EA KEYWORDS ARIES—**"Observe Separating Desires."

To connect with the evolutionary steps forward, we must honour the core need to be free to follow our instincts. Of course, balancing independence with consideration for others ensures we make progress now. This is a time to be centered, so that we can connect to the desires that help us with our lessons of equality consciousness.

**2nd GATE—EA KEYWORDS TAURUS—**"Self-Reliance & Self-Sufficiency."

Make sure to balance the need for self-sufficiency with a need to be happy in relationships. Spring is in the air and so we may be feeling frisky. Look around to see what is of value and consider what is needed to be more internally centered at this junction. Forward motion involves aligning with our higher values.

**3rd GATE—EA KEYWORDS GEMINI—**"Classify, Identify & Categorise."

The 27th degree of Gem/Sag correlates to the Galactic Center in our Milky Way, and to where our galaxy is headed in space. This sensitive degree helps us align with Natural Law. I recommend a course of study—a time of interaction with Nature. Naming the aspects of Natural Law is Gemini's gift. The Sagittarius polarity point invites us to embrace our Daemon Soul.

**4TH GATE—EA KEYWORDS LEO—**"Self-Actualizing Purpose."

The energies of the summer solstice at this juncture bring the Leonean desire for creative self-expression to the fore. It is an ideal time to balance our need for the Aquarius polarity of social integration. Avoiding the potential for narcissism, and instead using the strength of Leo's personal will to focus on our talent to connect to socially relevant themes, allows us to move forward now.

**5th GATE—EA KEYWORDS VIRGO—**"Subjective, Self-Orientation."

Virgo is a transitional time where the concerns of how to deal with guilt and how to use mental discernment are faced. While also deciding how to interface with the greater world around us, we must figure out our true place and right work. We are also collectively facing our sadomasochistic underpinnings—equal pay for equal work. Make time to meditate and take care of yourself to break bad habits now.

**6th GATE—EA KEYWORDS LIBRA—**"Objective Consciousness."
Libra is a time when a shift from subjective to objective consciousness takes place. As we embrace our social needs, on a New Moon/Venus, it is quite likely we will attract new relationships. We must learn to listen to others now. Some of the issues that might come up: Are we on a two-way street? Are we attentive to the balance of self-honouring and responding to the needs of others?

**7th GATE—EA KEYWORDS SCORPIO—**"Metamorphosis"

The phoenix rising out of the ashes and the snake shedding its skin are examples of the type of evolutionary growth we experience with the Natural Law of Scorpio. We could have a deeper spiritual or psychological awareness of how we are co-creating with God, but only if we have given up our need to control outcomes. To do so we must recognize that there are cosmic forces at play and we must learn how to align with them. ☯

# Seven Gates-Ascent of Venus 2018
## Venus Moon Conjunctions

| New Pentagram | 01/08/2018 | 18 CAP D | Sun-Venus Superior CNJ |
|---|---|---|---|
| Evening Star | 02/18/2018 | 10°PIS | Heliacal Set |
| | | | Moon Venus conjunctions |
| *Ascent* | | | **NOTES** |
| Gate 1 | 03/16/2018 | 14°AR | Meeting With The Goddess-Integration Of Self And Society Progresses. |
| Gate 2 | 04/17/2018 | 21°TAU | Adjustments To Personal And Social Limitations. Humility Or Humiliation. |
| Gate 3 | 05/17/2018 | 27°GEM | New Input & New Visions-Getting It Together To Fit Into The Social Order To Serve It. |
| Gate 4 | 06/16/2018 | 03°LEO | Atonement With The Father-Presentation Of The Talented Individual Is Well Received. |
| Gate 5 | 07/15/2018 | 6°VIR | Magical Flight-Light Workers, The ability to flow now with a higher purpose, or extreme stuckness. |
| Gate 6 | 08/14/2018 | 7°LIB | The Road Back-allows new patterns to guide the self to its place in the larger social context or universal order. |
| Gate 7 | 09/12/2018 | 2°SCO | Master of Two Worlds-Evolutionary Completion |

## JOURNAL YOUR SELF-DISCOVERY

| Evening Star | BALSAMIC PHASE |
|---|---|
| *Ascent* | Moon Venus conjunctions |
| Gate 1 | |
| Gate 2 | |
| Gate 3 | |
| Gate 4 | |
| Gate 5 | |
| Gate 6 | |
| Gate 7 | |

# Ascent of Venus 2018
## Evening Star Phases of Venus

| | | | |
|---|---|---|---|
| SUPERIOR CONJUNCTION | 01/08/18 | 19° ♑ | VENUS/SUN DIRECT |
| EVENING STAR | 01/16/18 | 28° ♑ | PHASE |
| HELIACAL RISE W | 02/18/18 | 10° ♓ | FAST |
| SEVEN GATES | MAR-SEP | 10° ♈ - 10° ♏ | FAST TO SLOW |
| GREATEST ELONGATION | 08/17/18 | 10° ♎ | SLOWING DOWN |
| GREATEST BRILLIANCE | 09/25/18 | 8° ♏ | SLOW MAX ELONGATION |
| STATION RX | 10/05/18 | 10° ♏ | SLOW |
| EVENING SET | 10/22/18 | 5° ♏ | STATIONARY |
| INFERIOR CONJUNCTION | 10/26/18 | 3° ♏ | RX NEW PENTAGRAM |
| NEW CYCLE | 11/01/18 | 29° ♏ | MORNING STAR |

| | | | |
|---|---|---|---|
| ♈ Aries | ♋ Cancer | ♎ Libra | ♑ Capricorn |
| ♉ Taurus | ♌ Leo | ♏ Scorpio | ♒ Aquarius |
| ♊ Gemini | ♍ Virgo | ♐ Sagittarius | ♓ Pisces |

| Name: | Phase: |
|---|---|
| **Points** | **Degree & Sign** |
| VPP 1 | |
| VPP 2 | |
| VPP 3 | |
| VPP 4 | |
| VPP 5 | |
| | |
| SUN | |
| MOON | |
| VENUS | |
| MERCURY | |
| MARS | |
| JUPITER | |
| SATURN | |
| | |
| URANUS | |
| NEPTUNE | |
| PLUTO | |
| | |
| NO NODE | |
| SO NODE | |
| M.C. | |
| I.C. | |
| ASC | |
| CHIRON | |
| CERES | |
| PALLAS | |
| JUNO | |
| ERIS | |
| VERTEX | |
| VESTA | |
| LILLITH | |

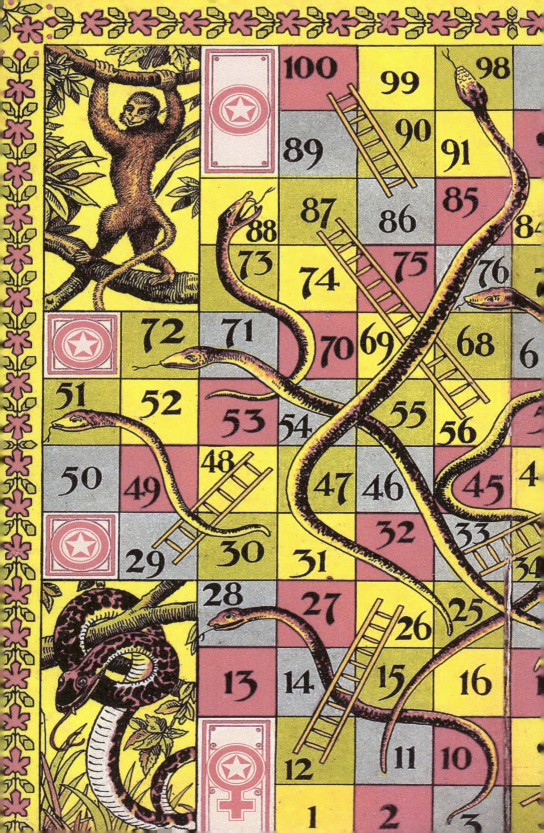

## PART NINE:
## 2019 WORKBOOK

Here are the tables for 2019 for the Descent of Venus as She transitions from Morning Star to Evening Star.

These specific tables which we have provided assist in allowing you to journal your experiences as Venus moves through the Seven Gates of the Gibbous, Morning Star Phase.

These EA Keywords are given to help you with the Natural Law behind the movement of the Moon and Venus.

Their Zodiacal positions for 2019 can be studied along with other years to find patterns, especially if the degrees of the transits hit a Natal or Progressed Planet within a small orb of up to 3 degrees for Venus and the Moon.

We encourage you to take a few years to study this phenomenon. If you are working with others, you will be able to assist them to delve deeper into Natural Law inquiries. ☯

# 2019 MORNING STAR—Descent of Venus

### 1st GATE—EA KEYWORDS SCORPIO—"Metamorphosis"

The phoenix rising out of the ashes and the snake shedding its skin are examples of the type of evolutionary growth we experience with the Natural Law of Scorpio. We could have a deeper spiritual or psychological awareness of how we are co-creating with God, but only if we have given up our need to control outcomes. To do so we must recognize the cosmic forces at play that are greater than ourselves

### 2nd GATE—EA KEYWORDS SCORPIO—"Metamorphosis"

Prepare to merge. These two months should bring change that is linked with growth. Marriage, commitment, sexuality and sharing are all within the domain of Scorpio. Facing issues of power and powerlessness is also often a part of our Scorpio growth patterns.

### 3RD GATE—EA KEYWORDS SAGITTARIUS—"Truth is Relative within Creation."

Sagittarius partners with the 2108 Ascent stage at 26 Gemini and the Galactic Center. It is a time for bigger planetary focus, so keep your eye on the big picture. In your own life embrace Natural Law.

### 4th GATE—EA KEYWORDS AQUARIUS—"Freedom From the Known."

Aquarius correlates to a time we may be dealing with anything we have repressed. We could also be choosing to rebel against the consensus, as we seek to individuate. With Uranus in Taurus, values and economic shifts may require your full attention now.

**5th GATE—EA KEYWORDS PISCES—**"God Permeates All Consciousness"

As we are learning to overcome victim/martyrdom and if we compliment more and complain less, we are more likely to see the perfection of creation. Pisces correlates to the desire to embrace God Consciousness wherein you recognize your interdependence.

**6th GATE—EA KEYWORDS ARIES—**"Observe Separating Desires."

To connect with the evolutionary steps forward, we must honour the core need to be free to follow our instincts. Of course, balancing independence with consideration for others ensures we make progress now. This is a time to be centered, so that we can connect to the desires that help us with our lessons of equality consciousness.

**7th GATE—EA KEYWORDS TAURUS—**"Self-Reliance & Self-Sufficiency."

Make sure you are balancing your need for self-sufficiency in your relationships. Spring is in the air and so you may be feeling frisky. Look around to see what is of value and consider how much you need to be more internally centered at this junction, so that forward-motion involves aligning with your higher values. ☯

# Seven Gates-Descent of Venus 2019
## Venus Moon Conjunctions

| New Pentagram | 10/26/2018 | 3°SC06' Rx | Sun-Venus Superior CNJ |
|---|---|---|---|
| Morning star | 11/01/2018 | 29° LIBRA | Heliacal Set |
| | | | Moon Venus conjunctions |
| **Descent** | | | ***MONOMYTH*** |
| Gate 1 | 12/03/2018 | 00° SC 39' | Call to adventure-narrowing of focus-direction |
| Gate 2 | 01/01/2019 | 24° SC 24' | Conflict as desire for more emerges |
| Gate 3 | 01/31/2019 | 26° SAG 21' | Opportunity for growth, action is externalized |
| Gate 4 | 03/02/2019 | 01° AQ 26' | Meeting the mentor, creative transformation. Receives a map or information |
| Gate 5 | 04/02/2019 | 07° PIS 45' | The need to initiate actions or forms before you can move forward |
| Gate 6 | 05/02/2019 | 14° AR 27' | Humility. The soul has a newly realized intention and must now analyze and adjust strategies |
| Gate 7 | 05/01/2019 | 21° TAU 11' | Equality. As opposition to one's ideas force oneself to face the others |

## JOURNAL YOUR SELF-DISCOVERY

| Morning Star | GIBBOUS PHASE |
|---|---|
| *Descent* | Moon Venus conjunctions |
| Gate 1 | |
| Gate 2 | |
| Gate 3 | |
| Gate 4 | |
| Gate 5 | |
| Gate 6 | |
| Gate 7 | |

# Descent of Venus 2019
## Morning Star Phases of Venus 2018-19

| | | | |
|---|---|---|---|
| RETROGRADE | 10/05/18 | 10°♏50'R | VENUS RETROGRADE |
| EVENING SET | 10/22/18 | 05°♏48'R | RETROGRADE |
| HELIACAL RISE E | 11/01/18 | 29°♎54'R | MORNING STAR |
| DIRECT | 11/16/18 | 25°♎14'D | VENUS DIRECT |
| GREATEST BRILLIANCE | 11/30/18 | 28°♎40'D | SLOW |
| GREATEST ELONGATION | 01/06/19 | 28°♏42'D | FAST |
| SEVEN GATES | DEC 2018-JUN 2019 | 00°♏-21°♉ | SEE NEXT TABLE |
| MORNING SET | 07/08/19 | 06°♋25' | SOLAR GLARE |
| SUPERIOR CONJUNCTION | 08/14/19 | 21°♌11' | NEW PENTAGRAM |
| EVENING STAR | 09/19/19 | 06°♎25'D | EVENING STAR |

| | | | |
|---|---|---|---|
| ♈ Aries | ♋ Cancer | ♎ Libra | ♑ Capricorn |
| ♉ Taurus | ♌ Leo | ♏ Scorpio | ♒ Aquarius |
| ♊ Gemini | ♍ Virgo | ♐ Sagittarius | ♓ Pisces |

| Name: | Phase: |
|---|---|
| **Points** | **Degree & Sign** |
| VPP 1 | |
| VPP 2 | |
| VPP 3 | |
| VPP 4 | |
| VPP 5 | |
| | |
| SUN | |
| MOON | |
| VENUS | |
| MERCURY | |
| MARS | |
| JUPITER | |
| SATURN | |
| | |
| URANUS | |
| NEPTUNE | |
| PLUTO | |
| | |
| NO NODE | |
| SO NODE | |
| M.C. | |
| I.C. | |
| ASC | |
| CHIRON | |
| CERES | |
| PALLAS | |
| JUNO | |
| ERIS | |
| VERTEX | |
| VESTA | |
| LILLITH | |

# PART TEN:
## 2020 WORKBOOK

Here are the tables for 2020 for the Ascent of Venus as she transitions from Evening Star to Morning Star.

These specific tables which we have provided assist in allowing you to journal your experiences as Venus moves through the Seven Gates of the Balsamic, Evening Star Phase.

These EA Keywords are given to help you with the Natural Law behind the movement of the Moon and Venus. Their Zodiacal positions for 2020 can be studied, along with other years, to find patterns, especially if the degrees of the transits hit a Natal or Progressed Planet within a small orb of up to 3 degrees for Venus and the Moon.

We encourage you to take a few years to study this phenomenon. After 2020 more tables can be found on my website: www.enlighteningtimes.com ☯

# 2020 EVENING STAR—Ascent of Venus

### 1st GATE—EA KEYWORDS FOR LIBRA—"Objective Consciousness."

Libra is the time when a shift from the subjective to the objective consciousness takes place. As we embrace our social needs on a New Moon/Venus—it is quite likely we will attract new relationships. We must learn to listen to others now. Some of the issues that might come up: Are we on a two-way street? Are our needs being met? Are we listening to the needs of others? Reexamine codependency now.

### 2nd GATE—EA KEYWORDS FOR SCORPIO—"Metamorphosis."

The phoenix rising out of the ashes and the snake shedding its skin are examples of the type of evolutionary growth we experience with the Natural Law of Scorpio. We could have a deeper spiritual or psychological awareness of how we are co-creating with God, but only if we have given up our need to control outcomes. To do so we must recognize the cosmic forces at play that are greater than ourselves

### 3rd GATE—EA KEYWORDS FOR CAPRICORN—"Responsibility For One's Actions."

This may be a time where we are held responsible for our actions so our self-determination is essential to our growth. We must also realize there are limitations, and we need to use our time wisely to accomplish the work our soul would have us fulfill.

### 4th GATE—EA KEYWORDS FOR AQUARIUS—"Freedom from the Known."

This correlates to a time we may be dealing with anything we have repressed. We could also be choosing to rebel against the consensus, as we seek to individuate. Collective changes, as a Retrograde Uranus informs us, may bring economic growth now.

**5th GATE—EA KEYWORDS FOR PISCES—**"God Permeates All Consciousness."

As we are learning to overcome victim/martyrdom and if we compliment more and complain less, we are more likely to see the perfection of creation. Pisces correlates to the desire to embrace God Consciousness wherein you recognize your interdependence.

**6th GATE—EA KEYWORDS ARIES—**"Observe Separating Desires."

To connect with the evolutionary steps forward, we must honour the core need to be free to follow our instincts. Of course, balancing independence with consideration for others ensures we make progress now. This is a time to be centered, so that we can connect to the desires that help us with our lessons of equality consciousness.

**7th GATE—EA KEYWORDS FOR TAURUS—**"Self-Reliance & Self-Sufficiency."

Make sure you are balancing your need for self-sufficiency in your relationships. Spring is in the air and so you may be feeling frisky. Look around to see what is of value and consider how much you need to be more internally centered at this junction, so that forward-motion involves aligning with your higher values. ☯

# Seven Gates-Ascent of Venus 2020
# Venus Moon Conjunctions

| New Pentagram | 08/14/2019 | 21° LEO 11' | Sun-Venus Superior INF CNJ |
|---|---|---|---|
| Evening Star | 09/19/2019 | 06° LIBRA | Heliacal Rise |
| | | | Moon Venus Conjunction |
| *Ascent* | | | *MONOMYTH* |
| Gate 1 | 09/29/2019 | 18° LIB 29' | Call To Adventure-Narrowing Of Focus-Direction |
| Gate 2 | 10/29/2019 | 26° SC 00' | Conflict As Desire For More Emerges |
| Gate 3 | 11/28-2019 | 03° CAP 25' | Opportunity For Growth, Action Is Externalized |
| Gate 4 | 12/28/2019 | 10° AQ 50' | Meeting The Mentor, Creative Transformation. Receives A Map or Information |
| Gate 5 | 01/28/2020 | 17° PIS 41' | The Need To Initiate Actions Or Forms Before You Can Move Forward |
| Gate 6 | 02/27/2020 | 22° AR 52' | Humility. The Soul has a newly realized intention and must now analyze and adjust strategies |
| Gate 7 | 03/28/2020 | 24° TAU 18' | Equality. As Opposition To Ones Ideas Force Oneself To Face The Others |

# JOURNAL YOUR SELF-DISCOVERY

| Evening Star | **BALSAMIC PHASE** |
|---|---|
| *Ascent* | Moon Venus conjunctions |
| Gate 1 | |
| Gate 2 | |
| Gate 3 | |
| Gate 4 | |
| Gate 5 | |
| Gate 6 | |
| Gate 7 | |

## Ascent of Venus 2020
## Evening Star Phases of Venus 2019-20

| | | | |
|---|---|---|---|
| SUPERIOR CONJUNCTION | 08/14/19 | 21°♌11' | VENUS/SUN DIRECT |
| EVENING STAR | 09/19/19 | 06°♎25' | |
| SEVEN GATES | SEP-MAR | 18°♎-24°♉ | FAST TO SLOW |
| | | | |
| GREATEST ELONGATION | 03/24/20 | 20°♉43' | SLOWING DOWN |
| GREATEST BRILLIANCE | 04/28/20 | 18°♊02' | SLOW MAX ELONGATION |
| RX | 05/13/20 | 21°♊50 | SLOW |
| EVENING SET | 05/28/20 | 17°♊23' | |
| INFERIOR CONJUNCTION | 06/03/20 | 13°♊35' | RX NEW PENTAGRAM |
| MORNING RISE | 06/10/20 | 09°♊44' | MORNING STAR |

| | | | |
|---|---|---|---|
| ♈ Aries | ♋ Cancer | ♎ Libra | ♑ Capricorn |
| ♉ Taurus | ♌ Leo | ♏ Scorpio | ♒ Aquarius |
| ♊ Gemini | ♍ Virgo | ♐ Sagittarius | ♓ Pisces |

| Name: | Phase: |
|---|---|
| **Points** | **Degree & Sign** |
| VPP 1 | |
| VPP 2 | |
| VPP 3 | |
| VPP 4 | |
| VPP 5 | |
| | |
| SUN | |
| MOON | |
| VENUS | |
| MERCURY | |
| MARS | |
| JUPITER | |
| SATURN | |
| | |
| URANUS | |
| NEPTUNE | |
| PLUTO | |
| | |
| NO NODE | |
| SO NODE | |
| M.C. | |
| I.C. | |
| ASC | |
| CHIRON | |
| CERES | |
| PALLAS | |
| JUNO | |
| ERIS | |
| VERTEX | |
| VESTA | |
| LILLITH | |

# AFTERWORD
## FROM AUTHOR TASHI POWERS

For so many of us on Earth, the movement of Venus caught our attention in the early 2000s when the tech revolution brought the phenomena called the—*Transit of Venus*—to the new frontier it was birthing.

This rare 1,215 year Venus event was bringing forth a new world order. The eight years from 2004-2012 gave so many new tools: tablets, the internet and iPhones were just some of this millennium's Kumari Kiss.

We were able to watch the actual movement of Venus on our smart phones as She marched forward, a small black dot moving across the Sun.

As I've come to admire the depth of Evolutionary Astrology I found we need more study on the Morning and Evening Stars in relationship to Venus's gibbous and balsamic phases. The Seven Gates are wide-open for a deeper look.

How is Venus intertwined in a cosmic embrace with Pluto? How does the VPP teach more about Natural Law? How do the Seven Gates affect us personally and collectively?

And as I researched that Venus' descent to the underworld actually correlates with Her being invisible in sunlight, it seemed even more reason to want to update Her ancient myths. Using my familiarity with the Monomyth I drew some comparisons to Venus's journey through all Her stages with Joseph Campbell's hero's journey.

The Planets speak to my Daemon Soul. A Daemon soul is a person who is deeply resonant with Nature. I can speak to the plant and animal realms and have interacted with subtle etheric realms since I was a baby. I feel like the Planets speak to all of us, and I want to know more about their beautiful spirals.

This study is just a beginning that is meant to stimulate our ongoing dialogue. It is my intention to ignite an investigation that allows us to include the Evolutionary Astrological principles of Natural Law into our study of the cycles of Venus.

I have added some photos to share with you, which I captured on my iPhone of the Angels, who appeared so brightly on my ceiling in the morning sun.

So in conclusion sharing, caring and inclusion are the basic tenets of evolution. I urge us all to embrace these Natural Laws so that the God/dess energies of Venus can once again be the natural path of Soul expression. ☯

Photo editing by Darius Gottlieb CelloHeart@gmail.com

**Bio: Tashi was born in a rain forest on the outskirts of Vancouver, BC. Her gifts as an astrologer were evident as early as 14-years-old, and she began reading professionally at 17. Her Venus is conjunct Jupiter on the GC axis at 28 Gemini. She has an international practice and is grateful to be able to share Natural Law with others.**

# LINKS
## TO HELP YOU EXPLORE THE MYSTERIES OF VENUS

### For more information on Jeffrey Wolf Green's EA
http://schoolofevolutionaryastrology.com

http://devagreen.com

### EA Glossary
http://schoolofevolutionaryastrology.com/evolutionary-astrology-books

### To join EA Zoom Meetings
https://www.facebook.com/groups/1673626642958879/

### *Links to articles and videos mentioned in the book*

https://www.youtube.com/watch?v=8p1CUe8w0AU

https://rosemarcus.com/rare-venus-occultation-june-56-2012/

http://kristinfontana.com/

https://astrobutterfly.com/2017/03/22/venus-conjunct-sun-a-new-venus-cycle-a-rebirth-of-the-hearth/

### Find more Venus dates here:

https://www.astro.com/swisseph/ae/venus1600.pdf

http://aastl.net/FindYourVenusStarPoint.pdf

http://cayelincastell.com/wp-content/uploads/2014/02/Venus-Overtones-from-1921-to-2042-wo-symbols.pdf

**Tashi Powers "Evolutionary Astrologer"**
www.enlighteningtimes.com

**VENUS PENTAGRAM MANDALA 2018**
https://www.youtube.com/watch?v=blBy-7HmU40&t=138s

**TASHI POWERS THE ASCENT OF VENUS 2018**
https://www.youtube.com/watch?v=2MxaXefiZkc&t=1877s

**ASCENT & DESCENT OF VENUS-MORNING STAR TO EVE-NING STAR**
https://www.youtube.com/watch?v=xunP108SHYs&t=10s

**MORE VIDEOS FROM EA ASTROLOGER TASHI POWERS**
https://www.youtube.com/results?search_query=TASHI+POWERS


**George Ozuna "Graphic Designer"**
georgeozuna@sbcglobal.net

**Photography of Darius Gottlieb**
www.artbliss.com

**Artwork of Leigh McCloskey**
www.leighmcloskey.com

**Nick Anthony Fiorenza**

http://www.lunarplanner.com/Images/Venus/pent%20drift.gif

http://www.lunarplanner.com/HCpages/Venus.html

CPSIA information can be obtained
at www.ICGtesting.com
Printed in the USA
BVHW091124311220
596843BV00006B/397